Relevance of Asian Development Experiences to African Problems

Seiji Naya
and
Robert McCleery

An International Center for Economic Growth Publication

ICS PRESS
San Francisco, California

Publication signifies that the International Center for Economic Growth believes a work to be a competent treatment worthy of public consideration. The findings, interpretations, and conclusions of a work are entirely those of the authors and should not be attributed to ICEG, its affiliated organizations, its Board of Overseers, or organizations that support ICEG.

Publication of this Occasional Paper was made possible by support from the United States Agency for International Development (AID) and the Starr Foundation.

Inquiries, book orders, and catalog requests should be addressed to ICS Press, 720 Market Street, San Francisco, California 94102, USA. Telephone: (415) 981-5353; fax: (415) 986-4878. Book orders within the contiguous United States: (800) 326-0263.

Library of Congress Cataloging-in-Publication Data

Naya, Seiji.
Relevance of Asian development experiences to African problems / Seiji Naya, in association with Robert McCleery.
p. cm. — (Occasional papers ; 39)
"An International Center for Economic Growth Publication."
Includes bibliographical references.
ISBN 1-55815-313-6
1. Africa—Economic conditions—1960– 2. Africa—Economic policy. 3. Asia—Economic conditions—1945– 4. Asia—Economic policy. 5. Economic development. I. McCleery, Robert. II. Title. III. Series: Occasional papers (International Center for Economic Growth) : no. 39.
HC800.N355 1994
338.96—dc20 93-50841
CIP

FOREWORD

This paper by Professor Seiji Naya of the University of Hawaii highlights the main findings of an Interregional Symposium on ''Promoting Accelcrated Development in Africa: Perspectives from the Asian Experience'' that the United Nations Department of Development Support and Management Services (UNDDSMS) organized in Abidjan, Côte d'Ivoire (June 15–19, 1992), jointly with the government of Japan and the African Development Bank.

Dr. Naya examines the postwar performance of developing countries, noting the high and accelerated growth of Asian economies in stark contrast with slow and even negative growth in Africa. From this comparison, the obvious question arises: Are there useful lessons that lesser developed countries in Africa can gain from development experiences in Asia?

The paper points to the key role of agriculture in providing the basis for sustained development in Asian economies; their emphasis on education, health, and human development generally in providing the means for accelerated growth; their ability to mobilize and channel savings into productive investment; and their outward-oriented trade and investment policies, which enabled them to benefit from world market opportunities. African economies in general were much less successful in dealing with these issues, and in closing the development gaps, as the paper points out.

From the Asian experience, the tasks that stand out for African policy makers are to enact policies which sustain macroeconomic stability, support agricultural and human resource development, provide incentives for savings and productive investment, maintain an outward-looking trade and industrial posture, and develop the human and institutional basis for policy implementation. The challenges are certainly formidable.

But as Professor Naya points out, there are no ''basket cases'' in development. Economic development is a long-term process; societies do not change overnight. Growth depends on how a country's physical and human resources are nurtured, managed, and utilized. Multilateral institutions and bilateral economic partners can and should play a supportive role. But ultimately African development depends on the African people. Just as Asians have turned former ''basket cases'' into dynamic economies, Africans face the challenge of putting their abundant resources to work in realizing their own visions of development and progress.

This paper, prepared by Professor Naya, who was himself instrumental in the substantive preparation and successful implementation of the Abidjan seminar and the Tokyo Conference, gives insightful policy directions toward that end. I trust that it will also be a valuable document in enhancing Africa-Asia development cooperation.

Ji Chaozhu
Under-secretary General
UNDDSMS

PREFACE

We are pleased to publish *Relevance of Asian Development Experiences to African Problems,* by Seiji Naya and Robert McCleery, as the thirty-ninth in our series of Occasional Papers, which feature reflections on broad policy issues by noted scholars.

The authors begin by noting that although the development experiences of some East Asian and Southeast Asian countries are the envy of the world, while the economic prospect for African countries looks dim, currently dynamic economies such as those of Singapore, South Korea, and Taiwan were also considered hopeless after World War II. The central question the paper addresses is whether African policy makers can learn from the Asian development experiences.

Authors Naya and McCleery first consider the histories and situations of Asia and Africa in regard to the four main gaps or challenges of development: the agricultural or basic needs gap, the human resource gap, the savings and investment gap, and the foreign exchange gap. Among the critical determinants of development performance, the authors emphasize macroeconomic stability, outward-oriented economic policies, investment in human capital, and development of small enterprise and the informal sector. All of these were important in Asia's growth and are serious problems in most African countries.

Asia also had the advantage of efficient bureaucratic governments, which worked in partnership with the private sectors to produce dynamic growth. An important priority in Africa, on the other hand, is to strengthen its countries' governmental and economic management capacities. Given the difficulties in developing such capacities, governmental expertise may continue to be a thorny area in many African countries.

The authors conclude with a list of ten recommendations to promote African development. Just as Asian countries benefited from the demonstration effect of nearby countries taking off on a successful trade and development trajectory, African countries can benefit from learning more about relevant Asian experiences. The authors propose programs to foster networking and visits between the two regions.

This paper was first commissioned by the United Nations' Department of Economic and Social Development and presented at the Tokyo International Conference on African Development, October 5–6, 1993. We are confident that policy makers and scholars will find it useful in their efforts to learn from the development experiences of other regions.

Nicolás Ardito-Barletta
General Director
International Center for Economic Growth

Panama City, Panama
April 1994

ABOUT THE AUTHORS

SEIJI NAYA is a senior adviser to ICEG and is chairman and professor of the Department of Economics at the University of Hawaii. He holds a Ph.D. from the University of Wisconsin and has been a faculty fellow at the National Bureau of Economic Research in New York. Dr. Naya has twice been the Rockefeller Foundation's visiting professor at Thammasat University in Bangkok, Thailand, and later became the chief economist of the Asian Development Bank. He has served as vice president of the East-West Center and as an adviser and consultant to such organizations as the U.N. Development Program, the U.S. Agency for International Development, and the Association of South East Asian Nations. He is the author of many professional articles and books.

ROBERT K. McCLEERY is an economist at the Research Institute of Economics and Business Administration, Kobe University. He has collaborated with Dr. Naya on the ICEG project *South Asia as a Dynamic Partner* and served as consultant to an ICEG project on human resource development and economic growth in Asia. Dr. McCleery's primary area of research and publication has been on U.S.–Mexico economic interdependence, including immigration reform and the North American Free Trade Agreement. His work has appeared in the *American Economic Review, Journal of Economic Perspectives,* and numerous edited volumes.

SEIJI NAYA AND ROBERT McCLEERY

Relevance of Asian Development Experiences to African Problems

Introduction to Asian Development: Myths and Realities

The enviable growth patterns of several Asian countries are well known. East Asia is the only region in the world that has been able to maintain strong, consistent growth patterns over several decades, led first by Japan and then by the newly industrializing economies (NIEs) of Hong Kong, South Korea, Singapore, and Taiwan. These economies have achieved not only two-digit growth rates and vast improvements in social indicators, but also very favorable income distributions. In the NIEs, the lowest quintile of the population receives more than 5 percent of total income, and the highest quintile receives less than 30 percent. From 1965 to 1990, incomes grew at 6 to 7 percent per capita in the NIEs and 3 to 5 percent per capita per annum in the newly emerging growth pole of Southeast Asia (Indonesia, Malaysia, and Thailand). By contrast,

This book publishes a paper commissioned by the United Nation's Department of Economic and Social Development (DESD) and presented at the Tokyo International Conference on African Development, October 5–6, 1993. The authors gratefully acknowledge Mr. Mikio Tajima of DESD for commissioning Seiji Naya to undertake this project and for his encouragement in carrying out the study. The assistance of Mr. A. Ould Abdallah and Dr. Mar Dieye of DESD is most appreciated. The authors would also like to thank Dr. Robert C. Young of the U.S. Agency for International Development and Laura E. Bailey of Innovative Resource Partners for their useful comments on an earlier draft of the paper, and Karen Eggleston for excellent research assistance. A summary version of this paper was presented by the senior author at the Consultation Meeting for the Tokyo International Conference on African Development in Dakar, Senegal, June 3–5, 1993. The views expressed herein are those of the authors alone and should not be attributed to the United Nations or any other institution.

the less developed countries (LDCs) on average recorded 2.5 percent per capita growth, and Africa only grew by 0.2 percent per capita over the same period (Naya and Imada 1992; Roemer 1993). In the first years of this decade, economic growth in Africa did not keep up with population growth of over 3 percent per annum, leading to a decline in per capita incomes of roughly 1 percent per year (Yaker 1992).

This book discusses some of the possible lessons to be learned from the Asian development experiences and their relevance for African development. We focus on Japan, the NIEs of East Asia, and certain Southeast Asian countries. In the interests of brevity, we may refer to ''Asian'' experiences. Nevertheless, it should not be forgotten that there are many poor countries in Asia: ''Asia has more billionaires than any other continent [but also] nearly twice as many people living in conditions of absolute poverty than the entire continent of Africa'' (Sweden Ministry of Foreign Affairs 1992, p. 43). Moreover, several Asian countries are transition economies, such as Mongolia, Vietnam, and North Korea.

There is no single Asian development model. This is even more apparent now than it was for writers in the early to mid-1980s, as first Thailand and Malaysia, then Indonesia and China, established their credentials as rapidly growing economies. Some of the success of the NIEs may be attributable to initial conditions and other fortuitous events, but the improved economic performance of the Association of South East Asian Nations (ASEAN) countries after adopting similar policies ''clearly attests to the importance of outward-looking policies'' (Naya and Imada 1992, p. 45). Economic development has taken place in countries of widely varying cultural backgrounds and under a wide range of political regimes—from democratic to authoritarian.

The diversity among the countries of Asia is as great as the diversity in Africa, in terms of population size, climate, resource base, and culture (see Tables 1 and 2 in the Appendix). Just as no single strategy was or could have been used in Asia, no single strategy drawn from the Asian experiences should be considered optimal for most or perhaps any African country. At best, we offer a number of recommendations for policies that might fit into an overall development strategy, a plan that must, to be effectively implemented, be embraced (if not designed) by national and local governments and bureaucracies.

The recommendations that follow are distilled from common themes in the development policies of Asian countries over their most successful periods. They are not meant to be panaceas or magic formulas. In fact, the adoption of any given policy without regard to the current policy environment may be as likely to hurt as to help economic growth. There is no substitute for saving more out of already meager incomes, working hard and productively for low pay, exposing domestic firms to competition from efficient foreign firms and accepting the fact that some will not survive, and taxing economic activities while encouraging risk-taking and profit-making.

When considering prospects for economic development, it is important to remember that there are no basket cases. No matter how grim prospects may seem for parts of Africa, one should take heart from the fact that such currently dynamic economies as Singapore, South Korea, and Taiwan were viewed as hopeless after World War II. In the 1960s, Singapore was regarded as Asia's Cuba. South Korea, devastatingly war-torn and divided, with its agricultural base bereft of the mineral resources in the north, nevertheless emerged within a generation of its civil war as a model of rapid and surprisingly equitable economic development.

The outlook is indeed bleak for much of Africa. But economic development is a long-term process. Societies cannot change overnight. Economies take time to grow, adjust, and develop. With Africa's abundant (though unevenly distributed and developed) natural and human resources, Africa can certainly build a more prosperous future.

In the following sections, we will first contrast the post-war development experiences of Asia and Africa with regards to the four main gaps, or fundamental challenges, of development: the agricultural (basic needs) gap, the human resource development gap, the savings and investment gap, and the foreign exchange gap. Closing or eliminating these gaps allows a country to grow according to its underlying potential (which may still be quite different in different societies).

The third section of the paper looks at differences in economic policies in the two regions and how those differences contributed to different outcomes. In particular, policies led to the closing or effective management of the four gaps in many—albeit not all—Asian countries and the widening of the gaps in most—but not all—African countries.

The role governments seek to play in their societies and what the populace expects from government will also be discussed. In addition, we touch upon the role of culture in economic development and the impact of external factors on domestic economic policies and performance.

The Four Development Gaps

The agricultural (basic needs) gap. Without exception, the success stories in Asia have been characterized by the rapid expansion of the provision of basic human needs—food and shelter—to the vast majority of the population. The proper development of agriculture and meeting the society's basic needs form the basis for filling the other development gaps, particularly the human resource gap involving nutrition, health, education, and training. Only a population with its basic needs met can be further cultivated as a resource. The burden on other resources of closing the agriculture and basic needs gap is directly related to the growth rate of the population (see Table 3 in the Appendix).[1]

Despite the widely known fact that growth in manufacturing exports is the single most remarkable feature of the performance of the dynamic Asian economies, agriculture played an important role in the growth of all but the city-states of Hong Kong and Singapore. According to James (1990), "the empirical record of economic growth and development in Asia over the past three decades convincingly demonstrates that countries neglecting agriculture tend to grow much more slowly than those that pursued agricultural development early on."

One critically important aspect of the success of Asian agricultural development has been land reform. In Japan, South Korea, and Taiwan, the implementation of agrarian reforms laid the foundation for agricultural development and more equitable distribution of the fruits of economic growth. A vigorous smallholder promotion scheme in Malaysia contributed to agricultural development. In contrast, several attempts at land redistribution in the Philippines resulted in "spectacular failure" (Hill 1993, p. 17). More successful Asian economies invested in the infrastructure, institutions, and organizations important for rural development and adopted realistic taxation policies so that "explicit or implicit taxation of agriculture was of limited extent or duration" (Naya and Imada 1992, p. 51). A sharp rise in agricultural productivity contributed to some or all of the following benefits for the dynamic Asian economies: (1) the release of labor to manufacturing activities in the cities; (2) the provision of foreign exchange (either directly through exports or through savings on food imports); and (3) the lowering of urban food prices, inflation, and thus pressures for wage increases.

The green revolution and its technologies were crucial for Asia, using the abundant water and labor intensively, along with fertilizer, to generate high yields and thus economizing on scarce land. Yet Japan and Taiwan (and, to a lesser extent, Korea) were successful even before the dissemination of the new technologies: "It's really the agricultural technology that the Japanese invented before the war that saved the Asian countries" (Peter Timmer in Roemer et al. 1991, p. 90).

Furthermore, Malaysia in particular has gone beyond a simple adaptation of new technologies developed elsewhere for tropical agriculture to develop one of the leading research programs and outreach efforts in developing or developed countries (Roemer, Tomich, and Vincent 1993). Other food products have been important since the mid-1970s, especially for Malaysia and Thailand, where income growth has substantially decreased the fraction of rice in total caloric consumption and increased demand for animal protein and feed (primarily maize).

> The Green Revolution in rice has attracted the attention of those who hope to derive lessons from the Southeast Asian experience, but it is important to note that other food crops also made important contributions both to increasing domestic food consumption and to exports. . . . It [is] clear that, particularly for Malaysia and Thailand, food commodities other than rice drove production growth: maize and cassava in Thailand and edible oil in Malaysia (Goldman 1994).

Thus, whereas Asian food production benefited greatly from the green revolution—which is not generally transferable to Africa without massive investments in irrigation, fertilizers, and pesticides and at a tremendous cost in foreign exchange—that is not the end of the story. Many of the policies used to increase yields in maize, edible oils, and other food products had more modest infrastructure requirements and may be more appropriate for Africa.

Table 4 lays out the contrasting agricultural performance statistics of Asian and African countries (see the Appendix). The three largest increases in food production per capita among all low- and middle-income developing countries from 1979–1981 to 1987–1989 were in Malaysia, China, and Indonesia, where policies conducive to agricultural growth were instituted or strengthened during the period. The cases of China and Indonesia, in particular, provide compelling evidence to refute the claim that macroeconomic reforms and openness only serve to benefit rich industrialists.

In China, for example, agricultural reforms begun in 1979 with the introduction of the "production responsibility system" transformed agriculture and greatly benefited rural residents. By breaking up the commune system, contracting production down to the household level, raising procurement prices, and allowing for market-based prices at the margin (after output quotas had been met), the agricultural sector was able to exceed a 7 percent annual average increase of gross value of agricultural output from 1978 to 1984 (more than twice the rate achieved over the previous two decades). Farmers' incomes in 1983 were 2.3 times that of 1979 in nominal terms, outstripping the growth of urban incomes, even though the urban to rural income ratio in real terms was still over 2:1 (World Bank 1985, pp. 9, 13). Although some top Chinese officials seem discouraged by the seemingly stagnant performance of grain output from 1984, overall agricultural output in China has continued to grow at a high rate; anomalies in the agricultural data or overemphasis on "the grain problem" should not obscure the fact that the household responsibility system has made and continues to make a remarkable contribution to China's agricultural development (Johnson 1990, pp. 116–19).

Policies that have been tremendously successful in generating manufacturing exports in Asian countries have spurred food production as well. The only caveat to this strong statement is that several other Asian countries that did not substantially change policies (for example, Laos and Myanmar) or began to shift only late in the period (for example, India and Vietnam) also recorded substantial, though smaller, gains.

The picture for African countries is almost completely reversed. Only four sub-Saharan African countries recorded any significant increases: Burkina Faso, Benin, Ghana, and Senegal,[2] and perhaps only in Ghana can the increase be directly tied to policy changes. Far more serious is the situation in the rest of Africa, typified by the performance in the world's four poorest countries: Mozambique, Ethiopia, Tanzania, and Somalia. In these countries, per capita food production dropped by 3 to 17 percent. While factors less subtle than economic policies—such as war—affect the figures for individual countries, the widespread decline throughout Africa is clear evidence of a net policy bias against food production and food producers, generally a numerous and already impoverished group. The consequences of the stagnation or decline in food production are increased human suffering and increased reliance on commercial grain imports and aid.

It is, of course, not crucial for all countries in the region to be self-sufficient in food production. There would be no problem, for example, if the stagnation in food production were due to African countries specializing in other agricultural products (such as coffee, cocoa, and cotton) in which they hold a comparative advantage and then trading with countries such as the United States (26 percent of the annual U.S. corn harvest is stored, not to mention the potential expansion of output if export demand increased). Yet similar declines in export crops were recorded in many of the same countries.

In sum, agricultural development in Asia provided the foundation for industrial growth. Agriculture proved to be a source of savings and foreign exchange for investment in other sectors, as well as provided income to farmers with which they could purchase manufactured goods. Taiwan's integration of agricultural development and industrialization is perhaps the most successful in the world (Roemer et al. 1991, p. 51). African countries may be able to learn from Asian development experience. Not all countries should strive for food self-sufficiency, but agricultural development should not be neglected.

The human resource development gap. Frequently one hears that social development and economic growth are in conflict. By competing for resources, they vie for priority among a country's long-term goals. Asian experiences show that this need not be the case; some countries have achieved both. The human development indicators of South Korea and Taiwan, for example, rival developed countries in many areas.

There are four basic issues in human resource development (HRD): how much of the society's resources can be devoted to HRD, how effectively those resources can be translated into services, how well services can be targeted to specific segments of the population, and how consistent the pattern of HRD is with the pattern of economic growth. To illustrate, let us consider the experience with HRD in several Asian countries.

Investment in people has been a focal point of East Asian development. One key has been the initial emphasis on labor-intensive industries, which, through raising the demand for labor, raised incomes and spread the benefits of growth relatively equitably throughout the society. High rates of public sector spending on HRD were augmented by considerable private spending, especially for education. In East and Southeast Asia, good infrastructure and well-developed institutions enabled human resource services to be delivered at a reasonable cost. No major segments of the population were passed over for reasons of ethnicity, gender, caste, or geography. Economic growth provided opportunities for newly developed education and skills to be utilized in productive employment; employment in turn provided higher incomes, a portion of which was spent to further augment HRD, thus forming a virtuous cycle.

In some Asian countries, parts of the cycle were either lacking or weak. High levels of spending on public sector enterprises and exorbitant defense expenditures squeezed out HRD in South Asia, with the exception of Sri Lanka and the neighboring Indian state of Kerala. Poor roads, lack of good communications, and a harsh geography made provision of basic services extremely costly in Nepal, Bhutan, Indonesia, the Philippines, and parts of India, Indochina, and China. Cultural attitudes toward women, the caste system, tribal peoples with indigenous languages in Southeast Asia, "border peoples" in Myanmar-Bangladesh, Myanmar-Thailand, Indonesia-Malaysia (Borneo), Indonesia–Papua New Guinea, and elsewhere, all contribute to unequal access to health services, education, and other aspects of HRD services.

Economic stagnation contributed to the inefficient use of human resources in the Philippines and in all of South Asia, particularly Sri Lanka. In the Philippines and Sri Lanka, discontent among the educated unemployed contributed to social unrest. (For the Philippines, emigration eased social problems and provided some return on the investment in higher education in the form of foreign exchange remittances.)

Health. In Africa, the health situation is graver than in virtually any of the Asian countries (see Table 5 in the Appendix). The infant mortality rate provides a good picture of nutrition and health care in developing countries. Every single low-income country in Africa is below average for the group of low-income countries, and thirteen out of twenty-four of these countries, including but not limited to the poorest, have more than twice the infant mortality rates of the group.

China and Sri Lanka stand out as countries whose provision of services related to health and welfare has far outpaced their economic development. In China, for example, between 1970 and 1990 life expectancy increased from sixty-one to seventy, and infant mortality rates declined while daily per capita calorie intake increased significantly. UNICEF considers China an example of "how the health, education, and welfare of children can be dramatically improved even at a low level of national income" (Sweden Ministry of Foreign Affairs 1992, p. 210).[3] In contrast, no country in Africa is immune from the charge that neglect of this aspect of HRD has hampered development efforts. Even at higher levels of income, African countries are often outliers, with infant mortality rates two to three times higher than in comparable countries (Côte d'Ivoire, Congo, Cameroon, Namibia, and Gabon).

One specific challenge in the HRD area is how to cope with the epidemic of acquired immune deficiency syndrome (AIDS) sweeping across equatorial Africa. In Zambia, 43 percent of soldiers tested positive for the human immunodeficiency virus (HIV), as did 36 percent of pregnant women. Thirty percent of supposedly healthy relatives of the AIDS patients, when screened for blood donations, also tested positive for the virus. In sub-Saharan Africa, one adult in forty is HIV-infected, as are nearly one million children (United Nations Development Program 1992, p. 14). The World Health Organization estimates that at least 6.6 million adults in Africa are infected with the

AIDS virus and that by 1994 the figure will have risen to ten million (Global Coalition for Africa 1992, p. 13).

While the rise in the death rate to date represents only the tip of the iceberg, deaths of people in the prime of life are already cutting into the scarce supply of skilled labor. To cope with the rising mortality rates, private companies and government agencies alike must train more employees and managers than they anticipate needing. Individual African countries and the world community as a whole must respond to this crisis. Although Asia by no means has all of the answers, something in this area too can be learned from certain anti-AIDs programs, specifically in Thailand.

Education. In terms of an educational system, what is needed in LDCs is a structure that starts by emphasizing primary, secondary, and vocational education. Over time, a country needs to increase the size of the pool of skilled labor and the ratio of skilled to unskilled workers. Skills can and should be developed not only in the classroom, but also on the job, through learning-by-doing. Japan, South Korea, Taiwan, Singapore—all these economies have reaped the rewards of investment in education, leading to highly skilled labor forces. In some countries, the educational investments have still not been enough, leaving the human resource gap incompletely filled. Thailand's investment in primary education, for example, has paved the way for development so far, but future progress is clouded by the lack of adequate secondary educational foundations.

Studies of the social value of education in developing countries identify primary education as the level at which returns are highest.[4] The percentage of the population completing at least a fourth-grade education is a guide to the capability of a country's labor force to perform simple industrial jobs requiring limited literacy and numeracy. Furthermore, education of females is particularly important. Information about family planning, nutrition, and health—including information on how to stop the spread of the AIDS virus—is most effectively transmitted to households through female education.

In terms of these basic educational levels, the picture looks a bit better for Africa than does the situation in health (see Table 6 in the Appendix). A few countries have an overwhelming majority of the latest cohort completing the fourth grade, even among the low-income countries (for example, Tanzania, Zambia, Ghana, Mauritania, Burkina Faso, and Niger), and others (Burundi, Rwanda, Cameroon, and Zimbabwe) are making rapid progress toward achieving that level. In contrast, several countries in Africa are experiencing stagnation or even retrogression in the provision of basic education to their populations. The pressure of rapid population growth is only one of several factors. In fact, the entire basic educational system in some countries appears to be in disarray or decay. These countries include Benin, Zaire, Ethiopia, Kenya, and Togo. Severe data problems limit the value of numerical comparisons. The basic problems may be more or less severe in a given country than the figures indicate, or just as severe in countries for which data are not available or are not as startling.

Most countries are making improvements in extending basic education to the female population. Yet there are still only about two female pupils per three male pupils in primary schools and one per two or three in secondary schools throughout much of Africa. Zaire is a fairly typical case for low-income Africa, with the ratio of female to male students rising from .48 to .73 in primary schools and from .15 to .43 in secondary schools between 1965 and 1989. In no country is the gender inequality in education increasing (with the possible exception of secondary education in Mozambique); only in a few countries—Chad, Benin, and Guinea—does female education seem to be stagnating at a low level.

Finally, an important issue in African human resource development is the brain drain from the continent. By 1987, nearly a third of Africa's skilled people had moved to Europe, impairing the capacity of African nations to govern and to train a new generation of professionals. Estimates put the drain of middle- and high-level managers from Africa at up to 60,000 between 1985 and 1990. In Ghana, for example, 60 percent of the doctors trained in the early 1980s are now abroad. In 1978 alone, Sudan lost 17 percent of doctors and dentists, 20 percent of university teaching staff, 30 percent of engineers, and 45 percent of surveyors (United Nations Development Program 1992, p. 57). Although there are no easy answers, it would be worthwhile to consider the experience of South Korea. That country successfully overcame its brain drain problem by actively recruiting back expatriate professionals. To do so, the salaries offered had to be reasonable and competitive.

With the exception of several low-income countries in South Asia, it is clear that Africa is starting at a tremendous disadvantage relative to Asia in the critical area of human resource development. The challenge facing both domestic policy makers and external aid organizations is daunting: to reallocate spending and mobilize new resources for HRD; to make the provision of services more efficient despite considerable geographical, social, institutional, and infrastructural difficulties; to target overlooked groups based on ethnicity, gender, geography, or religion; and to remove obstacles to labor-intensive growth. As Asia has amply demonstrated, rapid expansion of employment opportunities is the best way to combat poverty and inequality. Employment generates private savings and investment (including investment in HRD), as well as tax revenues for complementary public investment programs.

The savings and investment gap. The mobilization of domestic savings has played a critical role in Asian development. Those scanning macroeconomic data on the developing Asian economies are often most struck by the high rates of savings and investment in the region (see Table 7 in the Appendix). This was not always true, and, as will be illustrated in the next section, this achievement illustrates the importance of both macroeconomic stability and appropriate policies. Korea and Singapore increased their savings rates from 5 to 10 percent in the early 1960s to 37 and 45 percent respectively in 1990. Indonesia's savings rate varied from 0 to 8 percent in the mid-1960s before rising to 37 percent in 1990. Consistently high savings rates fueled and were further boosted by rapid growth.

In Africa, savings rates have been low and widely fluctuating, as illustrated in Table 7. There is a clear distinction between the haves and have-nots in terms of resources. Savings reflect resource endowments and vary widely with terms of trade shocks. The three richest countries in terms of marketable resources—Botswana, Gabon, and Nigeria—all exhibit routine fluctuations of about ten percentage points in their savings rates, with peak fluctuations of 18 to 20 percent (International Monetary Fund 1992). Such variance puts incredible strains on development planning and fuels boom and bust cycles, exacerbating the high level of uncertainty and risk characteristic of developing economies.

Conversely, the poorest countries in Africa save less than 10 percent of domestic production in a normal year and in a bad year consume all domestic production and much of whatever capital inflows they can generate. No fewer than thirteen African countries consumed more than 99 percent of their domestic product in at least one year since 1980, leaving themselves totally dependent on foreigners to finance (and direct?) their development. Obviously, rain-fed agricultural societies will be heavily dependent on weather; variability in rainfall is thus magnified in the savings rate, since savings is the residual of income minus consumption.

The need to mobilize savings for growth is critical in these countries. Rather than a problem of managing fluctuations, it seems to be more a question of creating something out of nothing. Yet even the poor save, though usually in the form of livestock, land, or seed. Often it is a question of how to develop institutions and institutional mechanisms that are *trusted* by the people to intermediate savings through a financial system. Where capital markets do not work, either through inappropriate policies or due to problems inherent in developing countries (such as high information costs), the expansion of economic activities for all but the largest private sector corporations can be accomplished only through self-finance. An entire economy attempting to finance growth through retained earnings cannot easily restructure or transform itself from an agrarian to a manufacturing-based economy.

Formal and informal financial intermediation. Studies indicate that three factors underlay the successful mobilization of domestic savings in dynamic Asian economies:

1. Positive real interest rates gave the populace incentives to save.

2. Sufficient availability and convenience of savings institutions, such as the postal savings system in Japan, encouraged savings and pooled resources.

3. The profitability of investment opportunities promoted domestic savings.

That similar policies are important for African economies is substantiated by Ikhide (1992) in his finding of a positive statistical relationship between real interest rates on the one hand and financial deepening and efficiency of investment on the other, based on a sample of sub-Saharan African countries. The government of a developing country has to provide incentives for financial intermediation so that the economy can move away from self-finance to utilization of financial intermediary institutions. Development of a financial system also depends heavily on the establishment of an effective regulatory system, so that financial soundness is maintained. Perhaps most importantly, financial reform and development require political commitment and macroeconomic stability.

In the formal financial sector, dynamic Asian economies have often implemented policies of financial regulation and credit allocation. Indeed, credit allocation has been one major tool of industrial policy, a tool that is still not obsolete. South Korea, for example, has been talking seriously about the need for financial reform for a long time, but even the financial plan of the reform-minded Kim Young Sam administration shows that administrators are loath to give up control of credit levers: "Even if the Kim administration holds to the reform timetable, it is unclear when banks will ever become totally independent of the government. . . . The situation could leave the government in firm control of the financial system" (Paisley 1993).

In many areas of Africa, less than 40 percent of the population has access to a bank (Nzemen 1989). According to Nowak (1989), "per capita bank credit in the private sector amounts to $48 p.a. [per annum] in sub-Saharan Africa, but 90% of the economic operators have no access to it" (p. 68). Development of the banking sector should be a priority for African LDCs.

Asian countries developed an effective substitute for working formal capital markets. Several Asian countries, most notably Korea and Taiwan, developed kerb (or curb) markets—the name evoking a street corner setting as opposed to a bank building. A local money lender could economize on the gathering of information related to the creditworthiness of a borrower by making the extended family responsible for the repayment of loans. Limited personal mobility in East Asian societies and a broad scope for individually tailored terms and conditions helped to make the system work. In Southeast Asia, for example, moneylenders, pawnshops, trade credits, and rotating credit associations performed an essential function for small borrowers; in some cases, governments tried to extend and adapt the state banking system to the requirements of these small borrowers (Hill 1993, p. 37). Throughout Asia, high interest rates in curb markets choked off demand for consumption loans. Borrowers needed good prospects for large profits to make the risk of lending worthwhile; thus the system contributed to allocative efficiency in investment.

African economies have also developed effective informal financial systems, such as the tontines of Cameroon, Senegal, Côte d'Ivoire, and Congo, also known as *esusu* in Nigeria, *likelemba* in Zaire, *susu* in Liberia, *cilimba* in Zambia, *chilembas* in Uganda, and *ekubs* in Ethiopia. Tontines form an informal financial market whereby members invest their savings and can obtain credit on a rotating basis. Tontines contribute to the monetarization of the rural economy, channeling otherwise hoarded funds into small-scale investments, which benefit from the collective monitoring by tontine members (Nzemen 1989). As in Asia, the interest rates are high: 50 to 90 percent for tontine members, 120 to 180 percent for nonmembers, with "credit facilities for small traders and purveyors of services often [involving] interest of 10% or 20% per week and sometimes per day" (Nowak 1989, p. 69). Credit is difficult to obtain, but risks are also high. Africa's informal financial institutions thus play a vital role in pooling funds and allocating them efficiently in underdeveloped areas.

Of course, informal intermediaries have their limitations: "Financial dualism aggravates economic dualism" (Nowak 1989, p. 68). There is no substitute for sound development of the formal financial sector, using such readily accessible institutions as the postal savings system of Japan. Nevertheless, in view of the relative success of Asian economies' curb markets, the role of such African informal financial institutions merits further study and encouragement as a partial answer for the mobilization and intermediation of savings in Africa.

Foreign aid and direct foreign investment. Foreign resource inflows allow countries to invest at a rate above that supportable by domestic savings alone. Of course, such inflows require corresponding flows of equity or debt; even official development assistance (ODA) may come with strings or conditionalities. Private capital flows follow investment opportunities, so they may strengthen economic development once it begins to take off. Yet private capital flows can also magnify boom and bust cycles, boosting investment when it is already high and exhibiting a net withdrawal of resources through debt service payments and withdrawal of equity when times are already tough. Concessional loans and aid should be countercyclical, but, in practice, hard times are strongly correlated with recessions in the donor countries; thus, ODA tends to be stretched more thinly at the very time that export revenues are declining.

Whereas foreign aid can be important in assisting economies to fill in gaps in savings and foreign exchange and can be channeled into extremely useful areas such as human resource development, these are only short-term solutions. In the long run, aid can only be supplementary; a country cannot depend on aid in the long term. The effectiveness of foreign aid in helping an economy launch its own sustained development depends critically on how the aid is used. Aid is ineffective when used to postpone needed reforms.

Aid did play a role in Asian development, and that role was positive mostly because aid was on the whole put to productive and efficient use. "Aid has worked in East Asia where it has augmented an increase in domestic savings to support much higher levels of investment than could otherwise have been contemplated and not worked in instances where it has substituted for a lack of growth in domestic savings (Korea 1953–60 and the Philippines)" (Sweden Ministry of Foreign Affairs 1992, p. 156). Aid can also assist in structural adjustment efforts. In the end, however, development must be internally generated.

Different countries and regions pursue different basic patterns of foreign resource utilization (see Tables 8 and 9 in the Appendix). Rapidly growing Asian countries generally drew in modest resources from abroad—about 2 to 5 percent of GDP—during their periods of high growth. Crises in this context are manageable, such as Korea's 4.4 percent fall in its savings at the onset of the second oil shock in 1980. Investment rates fell 4.3 percent in 1980 and another 2.2 percent in 1981, even though consumption had stabilized (International Monetary Fund 1992). Thus the decline in foreign resource inflows was modest and delayed; as a result, investment rates stabilized as a fraction of GDP and rapid growth resumed.

The worst Asian crisis in recent years may have been that faced by the Philippines in the mid-1980s. Savings plummeted from 26 to 21 to 16 percent of GDP in 1983, 1984, and 1985. Investment fell even faster—from 30 to 22 to 16 percent—as net foreign resources declined from 4 percent to zero, and the Philippines GDP contracted by more than 15 percent in 1984–1985. Nevertheless, the Philippines was able to restore a measure of investor confidence, leading to a repatriation of capital, a rise in investment levels to 20 percent of GDP, and a return to modest (3 to 6 percent) growth despite a continuing drop in net foreign capital inflows (−1 and −2 percent) in the next two years (International Monetary Fund 1992).

Indonesia also has had problems with its external debt. After defaulting in the mid-1960s, rapid economic growth and the oil boom helped Indonesia keep debt levels low until another crisis emerged in the mid-1980s, due to falling oil prices, maturing debt, and the rapidly appreciating yen (in which some 40 percent of the debt was denominated). The debt-service ratio approached 40 percent in the late 1980s. Indonesia avoided default by quick adoption of reform policies; a flexible donor response was also crucial (Hill 1993, p. 55).

The dynamic Asian economies have largely avoided onerous debt burdens; the key has been effective management of foreign capital inflows and flexible responses, both by governments and donors. Africa lacks both. Africa's debt is now larger than the annual regional GNP and almost two and a half times the value of exports. Whereas developing countries in other regions have received substantial debt relief, the debt crisis is still very real for Africa. Debt service consumes almost 31 percent of exports. There is need for a global initiative to address Africa's debt problems (Yaker 1992).

Poor management of foreign capital inflows in Africa has magnified the boom and bust cycle observed in savings. Examples include year-to-year adjustments in investment levels of 14 percent in Botswana, 11 percent in Tanzania and Zambia, and a remarkable 25 percent in both Gabon and the Congo (International Monetary Fund 1992). These figures evoke images of gold rushes to spend money on poorly planned and questionable projects, made more costly as scarce resources (including planning capabilities) are stretched too thinly or bid up in price, followed by half-completed buildings rusting to the ground, half-finished roads and dams abandoned, and other less visible testaments to good intentions gone bad. Why would a country attempt to invest 60 percent of its GDP in a single year, as the Congo did in 1982, given its level of economic development and absorptive capacity? Why would it borrow 13 percent of its GDP, over and above a healthy 47 percent savings rate, to finance such a spree? Alas, no better answer is forthcoming than that it was available.

The poorest countries for the most part rely on aid and lending to sustain double-digit investment rates. An investment rate of, say, 12 percent barely covers depreciation, with little left over to facilitate capital broadening to accommodate a rapidly growing labor force, much less to deepen capital to allow for improvements in the technological level of production and to fuel labor productivity growth. When one further considers that past policies have tilted the structure of production in the economy away from labor-intensive export activities and toward capital-intensive, state-owned industry, the picture is even bleaker.

Many Asian economies have been quite successful in attracting and absorbing direct foreign investment (DFI). Here again, patterns differ. Singapore welcomed DFI; South Korea preferred international borrowing. In light of the debt crisis of many African countries and the fact that few economies in the world could work their way out of debt as effectively as the Republic of Korea managed to, it makes sense for Africa to follow the pattern of encouraging DFI. Indeed, several African countries have already seen the wisdom of this approach. DFI is an important channel for receiving and absorbing foreign knowledge, including management skills and technology. Most critical in attracting DFI is the overall political and economic stability of the host country. Fiscal incentives, such as tax holidays and accelerated depreciation allowances, although widely used, are less important than a predictable policy environment and good infrastructure. In the late 1980s, for example, Indonesia did not offer incentives but attracted much more foreign investment than the Philippines, which did (Hill 1993, p. 41). DFI is also linked to human resource development, both because low human capital—in terms of health, education, and skills—lowers returns to investments and because a host economy's capacity to absorb the beneficial transfers from DFI relies critically on its human resource base.

Many African countries have begun to realize the importance of attracting DFI. Unfortunately, political and economic instability, sometimes corrupt and not impartial systems of justice, and overregulated policy environments in Africa do not inspire confidence among potential investors. In addition to addressing these fundamental problems, we would recommend that countries interested in further promoting DFI seriously consider establishing genuine "one-stop investment" offices.[5] By cutting through the red tape that foreign investors have to face, a country can go a long way toward enhancing its attractiveness to potential investors. Of course there is no substitute for basic political and macroeconomic stability, but policies to cut red tape and delays can help.

The foreign exchange gap. The previous section's discussion of foreign resource inflows in development as a complement to domestic savings draws no distinction between foreign and domestic currencies. In reality, however, most developing countries, particularly those whose currency is not freely convertible, ration foreign exchange. The government appropriates what it needs for debt service, defense hardware, and other needs at a preferential exchange rate; then the remainder is sold at a premium in a secondary market or, worse, allocated to licensed importers according to capacity, history, politics, or rent seeking. Under such a system, many inefficiencies develop. Imports of needed capital, intermediate goods, and raw materials are rationed to the private sector, introducing a further bias toward public sector production and against exporting, as the proceeds from exporting are usually captured by the government (purchased at the preferential rate). Thus, more important than gross flows are the extent of regulation in the foreign exchange market and the access of the private sector to foreign exchange.

The main feature that sets apart Asian countries is their emphasis on trade. Trade has been the engine of growth in the region. Country after country has promoted export-led growth strategies because domestic markets were not large enough for efficient import substitution development. Small city-states like Singapore and Hong Kong had no choice but to implement export-led growth; other countries such as Japan—and later Taiwan and South Korea—had a choice, but also chose export-led development. Most recently, ASEAN countries and coastal China, particularly the freewheeling southern provinces, have adopted similar policies, with similarly remarkable results (see Table 10 in the Appendix).

Outward-looking policies impose discipline on the domestic economy through international competition and market forces. The exchange rate and factor and input prices must be realistic in order to maintain export competitiveness. Openness therefore imposes an upper boundary on how much domestic prices can deviate from world market prices (Naya and Imada 1992, p. 48). The efficiency constraint of outward-oriented policies has played an important role in Asian economic dynamism. Successful export promoters have avoided overvalued exchange rates, devaluing whenever inflation threatened the economy's international competitiveness. Dollar (1992) shows that such policies have indeed made a difference in growth performance: "For the period 1976–1985, the most open quartile of countries had a per capita growth rate of 2.9%; the next quartile, 0.9%; the third quartile, −0.2%; and the most closed quartile, −1.3%." Among his conclusions is the estimate that a shift to an Asian level of outward-orientation in Africa would lead to a gain of 2.1 percentage points in per capita growth (p. 540). East Asian export promotion was extremely aggressive and relatively accepted in an earlier era of the international trading regime; Southeast Asian export promotion has been of a later vintage and perhaps more relevant for Africa.

African countries in general are smaller in population than Asian developing countries; therefore, African countries face an even greater constraint on industrialization if pursued through import substitution, relying on domestic markets. Export-led economic growth is thus even more important for African developing countries. The relative successes of export promotion in Mauritius and Zimbabwe, despite perhaps limited transferability, demonstrate that African economies can respond to similar policies. The record of former stars—such as Kenya, Côte d'Ivoire, and Ghana—underscores the fact that countries can go up or down. Among the countries that have shown a commitment to establishing export processing zones are Kenya, Liberia, Senegal, Togo,

Nigeria, and Tanzania. Of course, mere export promotion is not enough; success requires attention to quality and efficiency. Fafchamps (1992) notes that "Africa's rich artistic tradition can help [inspire the] design [of] products that are very appealing to western consumers and yet are differentiated from Asian exports" (p. 35). African countries would do well to encourage such exports as part of an overall package of outward-oriented development.

Filling in the foreign exchange gap involves a number of policies centered on flows of trade, investment, debt, and development assistance. The exchange rate is one key, as it affects the relative profitabilities of producing nontraded versus traded goods and selling in the home market versus exporting. But exchange rate manipulation does little good if private actors are insulated from the impact by nonconvertibility of the currency and/or strict licensing. Too often well-meaning policies to regulate the use of scarce foreign exchange result in a shrinking supply, as incentives to obtain foreign currency are curtailed. Thus both policies designed to increase the net inflow of foreign exchange and those designed to allocate it more efficiently should be considered.

In this area, it is especially clear that different Asian countries followed different policies, and different policies proved effective for different countries. In Korea, Taiwan, and even Japan, full convertibility was achieved quite late in the development process. The allocation of foreign exchange was controlled by the government, not through formal licensing but by subtle incentives and controls. Although this worked rather well in each case, the system depended on strong ties between the business and public sectors and on the competence—even "moral authority"—of the bureaucracy. The system does not seem to be transferable to many African countries; such tight controls have failed dismally in India and in a number of other developing countries. Indonesia and the Philippines each tried convertibility relatively early; Indonesia has not faced recurrent bouts of capital flight, while the Philippines has.

Exports were not the only source of foreign exchange for dynamic Asian economies. Direct foreign investment has provided additional capital, as well as technology and managerial skills. Open policies attracted DFI from Europe and the United States; more recently, Japan and the NIEs have invested heavily in their Asian neighbors, relocating "sunset industries" in labor-intensive manufacturing to Southeast Asia and China. This has been an important element of growth in the region (Naya and Imada 1992, p. 50). Local firms have learned quickly how to bypass multinational channels and work directly as international subcontractors, especially in the textile industry (Hill 1993). The African private sector must try to do the same with its incoming DFI. Labor-intensive industries from Asia have already begun to seek out low wages in some African countries. Mauritius hosts a good deal of recent investment from Hong Kong, and Taiwan is the leading investor in Madagascar (Winrock International 1991, p. 19).

DFI can be an important supplement or even substitute for high levels of debt. What is most important, however, is not so much the actual borrowing or investment, but how productively funds are utilized. In Southeast Asia, there has been a trend away from public debt toward private debt. African countries would benefit from trying to start a similar trend. Attraction of DFI requires a conducive environment, an issue to which we now turn.

Critical Determinants of Development Performance

Economic policies. Appropriate economic policies have been the key to Asia's development achievements.

Macroeconomic stability. Asia's economic success is based on macroeconomic stability, a feature sorely lacking in Africa. Macroeconomic stability is critically important, since it affects each of the four development gaps, as well as constituting a key component of structural adjustment policies. Most fundamentally, economic development is a long-term process that must be founded on macroeconomic stability. Long-term planning is too often held captive in Africa to crisis-mode operation; natural disasters, wars, and political instability demand attention and divert scarce human and physical resources, both domestic and foreign, away from long-term development planning and implementation. But as the Asian experience (particularly that of Thailand) demonstrates, maintenance of macro stability even in the face of political and socioeconomic crises forms a basis for economic development.

Stabilization begins with controlling inflation. The detrimental effects of inflation are numerous. Inflation inhibits the poor from access to basic needs and increases the dependency burden nonworking household members place on those who are employed. This in turn limits the ability of families to finance education out of savings or an individual to defer employment for education, despite the prospects of higher pay in the future. Inflation deters savers, who do not have access to financial instruments that earn positive real rates of interest, especially those accustomed to holding currency. It discourages financial intermediation by encouraging the purchase of unproductive assets as inflation hedges. It discourages investment by introducing additional uncertainty into an already risky environment. This is especially true where some prices are controlled by the government; a large element of investment becomes guessing when administered prices will be changed, and by how much. Rent seeking to influence these decisions is common. An important administered price in many countries is the exchange rate. Inflation erodes competitiveness by altering the real exchange rate, reducing the incentive to export. Unless the exchange rate is adjusted almost constantly, the widening gap between the nominal exchange rate and purchasing power generates expectations of a devaluation, which encourage foreign currency speculation if not outright capital flight, both of which widen the foreign exchange gap.

To control inflation, a country must manage money supply growth and the budget deficit. Monetizing a large budget deficit is the primary cause of double-digit inflation in developing countries. Asian countries were willing, when necessary, to sacrifice incomes in order to bring inflation under control. Only a few—the Philippines, South Korea, and Thailand—borrowed excessively, and the latter two soon corrected their mistake. In fact, policy flexibility, in the face of policy-induced as well as exogenous shocks, is an extremely important albeit underemphasized feature of Asian development (Hill 1993, p. 38). Policy makers must make hard decisions, both on how to allocate spending among conflicting economic and political priorities and on how to raise revenues to finance their spending plans. Both policy flexibility and allocating spending relate strongly to the role of the state, the topic of the next section.

The correlation between macroeconomic stability, as measured by average inflation, and economic performance is astounding in both Africa and Asia (see Table 11 in the Appendix). All Asian countries with inflation rates above 10 percent for the decade of the 1980s had rates of per capita GNP growth below 3 percent over the same period. In the Philippines, the highest inflation rate was coupled with the lowest growth rate. In Africa, countries exhibiting double-digit inflation had low or negative per capita income growth over the decade. But it is worth noting that only a few of the countries with single-digit inflation managed positive growth. Once stabilization is achieved, it still may take a push to get growth started.

Is there a lesson from Asia on how to get this push? It takes investment, and if private investors are reluctant, then a mix of public policy and investment designed to create opportunities for profitable investment in the economy is necessary. Policy makers must be pragmatic at such a time, suspend their opinions of what type of investment they want (domestic or foreign; in Asia—Chinese or Malaysian/Indonesia; in Africa—Indian or East African; etc.), and just get the ball rolling.

To avoid monetizing budget deficits, revenues must be raised. There are two points that often trip up policy makers in raising revenues through a process of growth and structural change. The first is the extension of taxation to the agricultural sector. There is a tendency to spare the agricultural sector from taxation. Whether for reasons of politics, equity, or cost-effectiveness (the costs of administering an income tax on farmers may be seen as prohibitive, relative to the costs per dollar of revenue of a trade tax), agriculture may be exempted. This policy leads to a number of unfortunate consequences, as it did in South Asia:

1. Farmers perceived that a subsidy was their due, and other government programs such as credit to rural areas yielded dismal repayment rates.

2. Structural transformation from agriculture to industry and services was inhibited, as one would be moving from outside to under the government's control.

3. In South Asian countries, where agriculture makes up about a third of GDP, the policy limits the tax base, but

in African countries, where nearly two-thirds of GDP is agriculture, the impact is unavoidably such a heavy tax on other sectors of the economy and trade that private, formal sector economic activity is minimal.

4. In the long run, the policy never seems to help the very rural poor it targets; instead the effect seems to be to keep them rural and poor.

5. The policy is devilishly hard to change once instituted.

East Asia had success by combining land reform with a taxation system that appeared to be fair to all, encouraging formal sector economic activity and not inhibiting the transformation from agriculture to industry.

The second point is the transition to direct taxation. The Asian experience indicates that there is scope to maintain revenue tariffs, particularly on consumer goods, until well into the development process. Thailand has average tariffs of over 20 percent, and Taiwan and Korea had many tariffs in the range of 20 to 30 percent until quite recently. Japan has still not fully liberalized its trade in some areas. Tariffs, so long as they are rebated to exporters, perform a useful function in encouraging production for export rather than the domestic market. What must be avoided is a system of nontariff barriers (NTBs) and prohibitive tariffs (with exceptions made for favorites), such as characterized India until quite recently. The conversion of nontariff barriers to tariffs increases both government revenues and the transparency of trade incentives. Many countries have learned that the only thing worse than wasting foreign exchange on the purchase of expensive foreign luxury goods is encouraging the inefficient production of those luxury goods domestically.

As part of trade policy, what is most critical is not necessarily the tariff rates per se—which may remain in the 30 percent range as revenue tariffs—but their dispersion. The dispersion of tariff rates needs to be reduced, so that the rates are more even across the board. Simultaneously, NTBs and red tape—such as collection invoices and required documentation—need to be reduced and streamlined. What is important is not tariff rates, but the cost of doing business. An argument can be made that reducing deadweight losses from slow customs clearance, delays in loading and unloading, etc., are even more important than tariff reductions, after the transition from prohibitive to revenue tariffs is made. For example, Singapore's success as an entrepôt for China and Southeast Asia may have initially relied on its low tariffs, but it has maintained or enhanced its position even as tariffs declined throughout the region by increasing its efficiency in customs, cargo handling, and other areas.

Converting NTBs to tariffs and reducing tariffs from "prohibitive" (100 percent or more) to "revenue" (20 to 40 percent) can allow the private sector to become better established before burdening both it and a fledgling bureaucracy with more complicated taxes. A corporate income tax and a value-added tax, along with a (normally nominal and self-reporting) personal income tax, are generally the best places to start. These taxes do not greatly distort important incentives for exporting, saving, investing, and improving technological sophistication. Value-added taxes were introduced in Indonesia in 1985 and in Singapore in 1993; Kenya has led the way in Africa with the introduction of a value-added tax in 1991 (Hill 1993; United Nations 1992).

At first, as reporting procedures and institutional arrangements are being developed and refined, tax inspectors may do little more than survey places of business, decide how much business they should be doing, and levy what is essentially a lump-sum tax (which is less distorting of incentives anyway). Of course, one must guard against corruption.[6] The Singapore system of a meritocracy, relatively high pay and status for government service in order to attract good people, and zero tolerance for abuse of rank or position may be relevant to Africa, although the system may take hold more or less easily in different cultures.

Structural adjustment and sequencing. Macroeconomic stability is the precondition for structural adjustment. Often it is considered an integral step in the process. Structural adjustment packages usually consist of three elements:

1. Stabilization measures, including good fiscal, monetary, and exchange rate policies that keep both the government budget and inflation under control

2. Corrections of distortions, including price, tax, and financial reforms, as well as liberalization, deregulation, and privatization

3. Institutional factors, building capacity to accommodate the economic reforms

Latter policies include the establishment of bank branches in rural areas, the setting up of a forward market in foreign exchange, and the development of an effective bureaucratic capacity for economic management.

In many respects it was not difficult for Asian economies to adopt such structural adjustment policies, since they are very consistent with the policies that were already in place. When policies advocated by the World Bank and other institutions conflicted with Asian prerogatives, policies were tailored to fit domestic conditions. For example, many economies have eschewed wholesale privatization of state enterprises. In China and Thailand, the issue of privatization is extremely sensitive. Policy makers have realized that they have to proceed slowly in such delicate and complex areas of the political economy. Structural adjustment policies thus have been adapted to local conditions and constraints, sometimes keeping intact the original intent and sometimes finessing the changes entirely.

Structural adjustment policies may have been easier for Asia, but they are essential for Africa. Macroeconomic stability and the usefulness of structural adjustment policies cannot be overemphasized. When suitably tailored to host country circumstances and sustained over a reasonable period of time, adjustment policies can have dramatically positive results. Although there is a common perception that such policies increase poverty (at least in the short run), empirical evidence from the Asian experience does not support this perception. The removal of agricultural price controls boosted rural incomes, and new labor-intensive export industries provided employment and incomes to low skill level workers. Structural adjustment need not exacerbate poverty. As Hill (1993) notes, "The fact that this conclusion holds in a country which reformed quickly and maintained growth momentum (Indonesia) and another where reform and growth were a good deal slower (Philippines) suggests that the structural adjustment–poverty nexus as postulated in much of the general literature is simplistic at best and wrong at worst'' (p. 66).

The sequencing of reform policies is another complex and delicate issue. Much debate surrounds the topic of proper sequencing. Taiwan's development experience gives one example of a reasonable and effective sequencing of reforms: after stabilization was achieved, the next steps were interest and exchange rate reforms, including unification of exchange rates and efforts to keep the exchange rate realistic. Taiwan liberalized the commercial account prior to liberalizing the capital account. Policies shifted from quantity controls to tariffs, maintaining a significant level of domestic protection while building international competitiveness in exporting industries and through export processing zones; only later did Taiwan liberalize imports (Ranis 1991, pp. 30–31). This sequence of structural adjustment policies was logical and obviously worked quite well for Taiwan. Different economies may consider variations in sequencing more appropriate to their conditions and capacities.

The entire concept of sequencing implies a degree of control over politics and policies by technocrats or economic planners not always found in developing or even developed countries. What is sometimes called a lack of political will to institute or sustain reform and adjustment policies may be inherent in factional or decentralized political systems. In some instances it may be best to grasp whatever opportunities for reform one can, whenever they present themselves, as opposed to seeking an ideal sequencing.

The informal sector. The macroeconomic statistics, social welfare indicators, and continuing policy failures paint a gloomy picture for Africa's future. The broad scope of the informal sector in Africa is both a symptom of the formal economy's problems and perhaps a ray of long-term hope. In 1985, the informal sector contributed as much as 34.6 percent of GDP in Liberia and 24.5 percent of GDP in Nigeria; it is estimated that in 1989 the informal sector employed 59 percent of the urban labor force (19 percent of the total African labor force) and contributed substantially to ongoing employment creation (Grey-Johnson 1992). Whereas employment in one- or two-employee enterprises involves mostly very low-paying and inefficient alternatives to formal sector jobs,[7] the broadly defined informal sector—including the informal money market—can play an important, positive role in economic development. The situation in some African countries is reminiscent in many ways of that of China in the late 1970s, India in the mid-1980s, and Vietnam today. Such similarity indicates that policy reforms comparable to those instituted in those countries could benefit the economies as a whole.

Informal sector firms gain many advantages that are not generalizable to the economy as a whole, such as tax avoidance; ignoring regulations regarding health, safety, and the environment; and even engaging in activities prohibited under certain civil and criminal laws. Expansion of the informal sector in Africa may be an indicator of overregulation by governments, to the detriment of incentives for production, distribution, and accumulation.

Motivations for regulation can seem innocuous. No one could object to the guarantee of a minimum wage sufficient to meet basic human needs, or to licensing requirements to allow urban and industrial planning. Yet in practice, politicians often impose a maze of regulations on hours, vacations, health, retirement, unemployment, and rights to unionization. Licenses are often approved and revoked arbitrarily or by rent-seeking bureaucrats. The consequences are too little entry of firms, too much market concentration, too little employment creation, and lack of incentives to work hard once a worker is employed.

The situation in Africa has been characterized as follows (Fafchamps 1992). The problem—poor work motivation and initiative. The cause—patronage and "defensive bureaucratization" in large firms. The result—self-employment in small, informal sector firms. Family labor minimizes supervision costs, allows flexible hours, and shares risks and returns. The informal sector hires dropouts who are unemployable in the glutted formal labor market. They receive training in exchange for long hours at low pay. When they have learned enough, they go into business for themselves, continuing the cycle with their own family members and apprentices. Small businesses can thrive in areas like artisanship, micro retailing, and money lending, where informational advantages more than offset any scale economies. These firms are frequently the only outlet for small investors seeking better returns than those available in the regulated banking system. For example, civil servants might invest in the business activities of less-educated family members.

African governments have often persecuted the informal sector. Avoidance of regulation, arbitrage, and speculative activities draw the ire if not the fire of the local authorities. Efforts to control or restrain such trade have included bulldozing of markets, setting up roadblocks, and executing suspected black marketeers. One feature of the informal sector that draws such bureaucratic ire is its perceived tax evasion. As Oyowe (1993) points out, however, under the tax exemption thresholds for low-income levels, much of the informal sector would be exempt from taxation anyway, since even small business owners' incomes are extremely low and unstable (p. 80).

A few recommendations for policy changes worth African officials' consideration regarding the informal sector are as follows:

1. Foster a change of attitude toward the informal sector and acceptance of the sector as a resource to the economy.

2. Streamline and reform business registration and licensing for health, safety, and environmental concerns. Currently, officials have and exercise the authority to close firms down, or threaten to do so, unless bribes and patronage are forthcoming. There are many obstacles to a successful business-government partnership for economic development, including historical animosity, ethnic and tribal divisions, and innumerable jealousies. Accommodation is necessary. Much can be learned from the Asian experience of government-business relations, discussed next.

3. Extend government credit, training, and other services to the informal sector, to help firms compete on a more equal footing, while simultaneously deregulating the economy as a whole.

4. Help informal sector firms develop trader-producer linkages, obtain subcontracting agreements, and gain access to informational economies. Important in this regard is the role of private traders linking small domestic producers

> to foreign suppliers and markets. Ideally, some processes will be standardized and mechanized; but the role of small subcontractors will continue to expand. These policies are along the line of a Taiwan model of export development. As Fafchamps (1992, p. 33) notes, "What Africa perhaps needs most is an active trading class well versed in international trade." Here again the crucial significance of human resource development comes to the fore.

The role of the government. The private sector should serve as the engine of growth and the implementer of the development vision. The importance of the private sector, however, does not diminish the role of the government in economic development. Letting the private sector be the engine of growth does not equate with the Western idea of laissez-faire. The governments of all of the dynamic Asian economies (except Hong Kong) played a much larger role than that dictated by neoclassical economics, i.e., the provision of public goods and the correction of market failure. Asian governments played a crucial role in their economies by creating factors conducive to the working of the private sector.

In contrast, African states have not fostered private–public sector cooperation enough. Olowu (1993) notes that African states "must not repress but encourage private sector initiatives. . . . As the experience of the Asian countries shows, the state must help to reduce uncertainty faced by private entrepreneurs . . . [as well as] create a regulatory regime that fosters domestic and international assistance to small scale businesses in the informal sector [and] maintain law and order . . ." (p. 5). Whereas Japan and South Korea promoted large business conglomerates (known as *zaibatsu* and *chaebol*), Taiwan fostered development of small and medium-sized businesses in the private sector (large enterprises have often been controlled by the Taiwanese government). Given African bureaucratic capacities, one important role of African governments would be to follow the Taiwanese model in terms of promoting small and medium-sized private enterprises.

Asian economies have been the beneficiaries of relatively efficient and disciplined government bureaucracies. The "high degree of professionalism in the ranks of the civil service" in the NIEs (James, Naya, and Meier 1989, p. 211) has been critical in enabling close government-business relationships to remain growth-stimulating instead of corrupt and growth-inhibiting. The role of government in East Asia also went beyond an autonomous bureaucracy to one of close partnership between government and business: "In the Asian form of capitalism, a positive relationship exists between the business community and the government. Instead of the adversarial relationship often found in the West, there is a hierarchical relationship in East and Southeast Asia where the government may directly influence the conduct of private enterprises for the benefit of the public good, and, in turn, government is expected to assist and protect the private enterprises. . . . Close collaboration helps to ensure that appropriate policies are adopted and that a constituency supporting these policies exists. A cozy relationship between government and business can invite corruption, however, and thus care should be taken to maintain accountability of public officials" (Naya and Imada 1992, p. 54). The latter point is underscored by the myriad political corruption scandals currently reverberating throughout the Japanese and South Korean political economies. One must also beware of government-business ties leading to an abdication of the government's role in protecting consumers from unsafe products and collusive pricing. Nevertheless, close government-business relationships can and have provided important benefits for development: "Government support in the context of an outward-looking strategy helps to encourage risk taking and innovation by business. The hierarchical relationship allows for coordinated and timely responses to unforeseen contingencies" (James, Naya, and Meier 1989, p. 211).

What is important is the role the government plays, not its absolute size (see Tables 12 and 13 in the Appendix). Too much emphasis is placed on the size of government. In Asia, the successful Thai government, the unsuccessful Philippine government, and the extremely successful Korean government are the smallest as a percentage of GNP. At the other end of the spectrum, the successful Malaysian government, the unsuccessful Papua New Guinean government, and the extremely successful Singaporean government are the largest. Seven of the thirteen African countries for which data are available are in the 15 to 30 percent range defined by the aforementioned Asian countries. Of the six that are not, three are "too high" and three are "too low." Much more emphasis should be placed on what government does, how well it does it, and how it finances its activities.

A government needs to set forth the long-term vision for development and to establish a rule of law that is simple and as transparent as possible. Another critical role is establishing good macroeconomic policies and intervening to make the market work rather than intervening to destroy market mechanisms. Several East Asian countries have implemented industrial policies, utilizing tools of financial control, tariffs and quotas, weak antitrust laws, favoritism in government procurement, and administrative "guidance" by such institutions as Japan's Ministry of International Trade and Industry and South Korea's Economic Planning Board. More recently, industrial policy has focussed more on a research and development basis for selecting sectors, rather than direct intervention. Successful industrial policy depends upon a strong, effective bureaucracy, as well as a special government-business relationship; the transferability of this aspect of Asian development, therefore, may be limited. Southeast Asian countries have demonstrated that industrial policies are not indispensable ingredients in outward-oriented development success stories.

A more important feature of successful Asian development has been the ability to recognize mistakes and to correct defective policies. Singapore, for example, tried to raise wages excessively in the mid-1980s, but soon realized the folly of trying to hasten a market process. South Korea, also, when it instituted policies speeding up the development of chemical and heavy industries in the late 1970s and early 1980s, soon recognized that its policies were driving beyond the markets' abilities to absorb and that they had to revert to earlier policies.

In attempting to define an appropriate role for the government, it must be remembered how inexperienced Africa is in self-governance. The bureaucracies are weak; there is limited indigenous capability for planning, formulating, and implementing policies. Yet the private sector is in many ways no more developed. And the relationship between the two sectors ranges from sheer hostility to close but inefficient cooperation—for example, in capturing domestic markets in monopolistic or oligopolistic ways (Winrock International 1991, p. 140). Attitudes need to change, and productive cooperation must be fostered. In addition, an argument can be made that both the public sector and the private sector should focus their attention and talents on an extremely limited number of tasks.[8] These tasks would quite rightly differ from country to country. It may be that a blanket statement such as "African governments should specialize in the provision of transportation and irrigation infrastructure" may be as limiting as "African economies should specialize in the production of garments."

Rather than reserving sectors for government activity, policy makers should be looking for effective cooperation in a number of traditional and innovative new areas. Cooperation with the private sectors has worked extremely well for some Asian countries. Cooperation with multinational corporations in the building of needed infrastructure in a build-operate or build-operate-transfer mode could hasten development while economizing on spending and foreign exchange. Even in the areas of health, nutrition, and basic education, scope exists to expand cooperation with nongovernmental organizations (NGOs) and donors. Following this line of thinking, African governments are not so much too big as they are overcommitted. The ultimate goal of this strategy for both African countries and donors must be to build capacity for effective analysis and action in Africa.

In Asia, not only have individual governments tended to define their appropriate role narrowly and to stick to that definition in the face of pressures to solve all of the country's ills, but regional institutions have also contributed to economic growth by playing a limited and appropriate role. ASEAN has often been termed a failure from the perspective of economic integration. But economic integration was never its intent. In many ways, its rhetoric on economic issues was an excuse to forge political and security ties in the region. This in turn has yielded economic benefits to its member countries. Defense spending as a percentage of GDP dropped, particularly in Indonesia and Singapore, where it declined from 19 and 35 percent respectively in 1972 to 8 and 22 percent in 1990 (see Table 13 in the Appendix). Data for Africa is much more sketchy, but casual evidence suggests that ratios in excess of 20 percent are common, and no similar reduction in defense spending is evident. According to (low) official statistics, "an estimated 4.8% of GDP is used for defense in Sub-Saharan Africa, compared with 3.6% in South Asia and 1.6% in Latin America" (Global Coalition for Africa 1992, p. 6). Regional institution building, aided by U.N. initiatives, could help in this area, allowing a shift in expenditures toward investments in human and physical capital.

In Asia, as countries have become interdependent, increasing interaction has taken place not only between the government and the private sector, but also between all kinds of professionals. Because neighboring countries have all adopted outward-oriented policies, international meetings of scholars and policy makers within the region have become more and more frequent. Often policy makers are themselves scholars and move back into academic circles after serving as statesmen. With frequent meetings between professionals on policy issues, much cross-fertilization takes place. Bad economic policies become difficult to justify. This kind of interaction needs to be fostered in Africa as well. One effective way to build capacity in Africa, and at more than just the overall institutional level, would be to support such professional interactions on a broad scale. An important side effect of such professional interactions is the demonstration effect of both good and bad policies. Initially, multilateral institutions such as the World Bank and the United Nations can play an important role in facilitating meetings of professionals and strengthening bureaucracies.

Cultural factors. In the 1980s, a number of debates broke out on the topic of the relative importance of cultural factors versus economic policies in the determination of economic growth rates. Those who argued for the importance of cultural factors made a good point, that "Eastern capitalism" is fundamentally different from "Western capitalism," and thus a Western-centered perspective is not adequate (Berger and Hsiao 1988). Rather than resting the argument on the formal Confucian traditions of Asia (which had earlier been held responsible for the slow growth rates of China, Singapore, and Taiwan), they defined a more pragmatic post-Confucianist culture, augmented by Buddhist, Shinto, and numerous folk religions.

Our position is that culture is indeed important, as economic incentives and motivations are certainly not the only determinants of behavior. While not to ignore cultural factors, we have now seen countries in Southeast Asia and even South Asia fundamentally change the direction and nature of their economic policies, and, apparently as a result, jump from a low to a high growth path. "Some have argued that Confucianism, which encourages hard work, saving, and education, has been an instrumental factor [in Asian development], and indeed it has. High rates of savings permitted domestic expansion without large external debts. The emphasis on education created a large pool of literate and skilled workers able to meet the needs of an industrializing economy. But these characteristics are not confined to those with the Confucian ethic" (Naya and Imada 1992, p. 56). Cultural differences between countries such as Korea, Taiwan, Indonesia, and India (and even within countries such as Malaysia, Singapore, Indonesia, and India), and sharp changes in economic performance following policy changes within a country, invalidate the claim that the economic success in Asia is dependent on a common, homogeneous culture. It is clear that what changed in the late 1980s in India, in the mid-1980s in Indonesia, in the late 1970s in China, and in the early to mid-1960s in Korea and Taiwan was not the culture (which can evolve and change, but not rapidly), but economic policies.

We can now demonstrate fairly conclusively the importance of economic policies in explaining why long-term growth rates have differed among countries with relatively similar endowments and in a given country in different periods. Yet it may be true that cultural factors determine how responsive an economy is to economic policy changes, or why eliminating the four gaps may produce (hypothetically) 10 percent long-term growth in China and 6 percent growth in Indonesia. We hint at areas for future study by hypothesizing that social and cultural factors affect the cost of providing a given amount of human resource development, influence the prospects for institution building and use of informal mechanisms in areas traditionally subject to market failures in developing countries (such as the kerb market for credit), and affect the response to policy stimulus.[9] These questions deserve careful study by scholars knowledgeable in these areas.

External factors. It is important to recognize that each Asian success story took place in a specific global context. Even as the link between stimulus and response in the physical sciences may be dependent on the environment (altitude, temperature, etc.), the link between economic policies and results may also be dependent on the specific global economic environment. Having stated this, one is struck by the variance in the economic situation in which different waves of Asian countries successfully pursued economic growth through policies that were hardly identical, but seem much more similar than the global context in the 1960s, 1970s, 1980s, and early 1990s. Rather than being able to dismiss the Asian success stories as being a product of their specific environment and thus having little relevance for countries today, the remarkable fact is how consistently these countries recorded high rates of growth in manufactured exports and GDP despite changes in their environment. Through the high-growth 1960s; the commodity price boom, inflationary bouts, and low interest rates of the 1970s; and the high interest rates, exchange rate realignments, and slow growth in output and world trade volumes in the 1980s; Asian countries have continued to grow. Expanding market shares have substituted for rapid world trade growth; prudent policies have limited the impact of interest rate fluctuations; and the flexibility of policy makers and firms alike have helped Asian economies to change with rapidly changing circumstances.

The chief fear of the 1990s seems to be that the end of the cold war will spawn a new protectionism in developed countries. Indeed, a cursory look at recent trade policies and conflicts in the United States and Europe seems to support that view. Yet one must also consider the recent success of China, India, Indonesia, and Pakistan in expanding their manufactured exports at rates varying from 10 to over 30 percent per year in the early 1990s. For the determined exporters, there are in fact more markets available now: ''Not only are there the US and the EC, but also the NIEs themselves, a resurgent Latin America, and Eastern Europe'' (Winrock International 1991, p. 19). While it may well be more difficult to penetrate developed country markets in the future, alternatives to a more outward-oriented and open economy have failed to deliver either economic growth or substantial improvements in the lot of the common people over the long run. Rather than increasing vulnerability to external shocks, the policy mix in Asia seems to promote adaptability to changing circumstances in the global economy. Aside from the clear connections between high human resource development, a competent bureaucracy, and openness to information and technology from abroad (not just price signals), this link is rather complex and worthy of further study.

We have described a number of "virtuous cycles" in the development process of a single country; for instance, increased investment, increased income, increased savings, increased investment in HRD, increased complementary investments in human and physical capital, increased economic activity, increased tax collections (which can be used in part for further HRD expenditure), etc. The following short section will attempt to quantify how a virtuous cycle can develop for a region, building on what is often termed the "demonstration effect," and how countries can be left out (for example, the Philippines).

Successful development in one country can lead to the emulation of those policies identified (by either the leader or follower country) as instrumental to economic development. It is hypothesized that the strength of the demonstration effect is directly proportional to distance, where "distance" may be defined beyond mere geography to include ethnic, religious, and other cultural factors. Yet two other less widely recognized factors may be just as important: the leader economy's direct pull on regional trade and investment flows and the flow of ideas and information through ministerial and subministerial meetings in regional forums (for Asia: the Association of South East Asian Nations, the Asia-Pacific Economic Cooperation, the Pacific Economic Cooperation Conference, the Pacific Basin Economic Council, etc.).

Rapid economic growth in a country provides an opportunity for neighboring countries to be pulled along, through increased trade—including tourism and other services—and investment flows. Fast growth means increased demand for raw materials, components, and consumer goods from all trading partners, but with a natural bias toward neighboring countries (based on transportation cost and time advantages; greater information about products, cost, and quality; common tastes; and often well-developed regional supply relationships). Rapid growth also involves restructuring the economy. In Asia, this meant spinning off industries in which comparative advantage was falling to neighboring countries at the appropriate level of development. For Japan, first textiles and then simple electronics, and finally capital- and space-intensive manufacturing (such as some chemical and metal processing) moved abroad as first labor then land became relatively expensive. The extent to which this phenomenon actually occurs depends on the strength of regional bias and of the lead country's reliance on external suppliers and markets, but primarily on the degree of outward orientation in the follower countries, especially receptiveness to foreign investment and policies affecting exports. The inducement for policy change is thus not merely the fact that a neighboring country is growing rapidly, but also the opportunity to ride on its coattails to more rapid growth.

Similarly, a follower country is more likely to make policy changes in response to a successful development if (1) the context and implementation of the policy are well understood; (2) questions about the impact of the potential policy shift on different groups can be asked and answered in advance; and (3) if there is someone to consult with in the event that problems develop during the planning or implementation stages. What better way is there to develop the personal contacts among mid- and upper-level bureaucrats and policy makers in the region than through regional and subregional meetings? ASEAN, for instance, was initially criticized for having too many meetings, with too little tangible output. But very important intangible outputs have been developed in the form of personal friendships, good working relationships, and a growing policy consensus.

Once again, the implications for African development and the U.N.'s role are not straightforward. Some observers have used the demonstration effect logic to argue for the concentration of development resources in one or two especially promising countries, to engineer regional successes in Africa. But would this work? The supporting conditions appear to be weak. Traditional trade links are with European countries; transportation costs within the region are quite high (for instance, direct air freight routes between African countries are uncommon, requiring long layovers or transshipment through Europe); and (at least initially) growth would not be outward-oriented. The exchange of information and personal networks present in ASEAN also seem to be lacking, despite the best efforts of the Economic Community of West African States and other regional forums. The U.N. can help to build these links.

Conclusions and Recommendations

Economic development is a long-term process. Looking at the dynamic Asian economies of today, it is hard to imagine that they were once considered basket cases, but they were. The present African crises of starvation, civil war, natural disasters, collapsing economies, and unacceptable human suffering do indeed make the future seem bleak. But an old Chinese proverb reminds us that "it is often darkest right before dawn." The potential for change and progress in Africa is there.

Unlocking Africa's potential requires effective economic policies. The Asian development experience points to several critical policy areas for sustainable development:

1. Macroeconomic stability
2. Agricultural development
3. Human resource development
4. Mobilization of savings, development of financial intermediation, and incentives for productive investment
5. Outward-orientation and attraction of DFI
6. Effective management of foreign exchange resources and incentives to potential producers of foreign exchange
7. Proper sequencing of structural adjustment policies
8. Institutional capacity building and attention to the problem of governance
9. Development of the informal sector
10. Encouragement of a dynamic private sector working in cooperation with government toward a society-wide vision of development

What we are saying is not new. Most of the policy prescriptions are familiar both to economists and policy makers. Quotes from famous economists are beginning to sound alike, although they are expressed with varying degrees of cohesiveness, depth, and conditionality.[10]

Donors need to help Africa build capacity for effective economic management. Although humanitarian aid and short-term assistance are necessary, the focus needs to be put on building institutional capacity. We have proposed that programs to foster networking between the policy makers and development scholars of Africa also be given priority. One effort to monitor closely—and perhaps build upon—is the African Capacity Building Foundation, a joint initiative of the United Nations and concerned African institutions. Begun in 1991 and funded by a consortium of donors and African governments, the foundation will focus, at least initially, on the key areas of policy analysis and development management.

In addition, there is no reason why the Asian experience of successful economic development and its relevance for Africa has to be mediated by Western scholars. Programs should be established to foster direct interactions between Africans and Asians. We propose the development of scholarships and training programs to sponsor visits by African policy makers to Japan, China, the NIEs, and other Asian countries to learn firsthand of their development experiences. Attention should be given not only to government policy, but also to private sector dynamism and how the two sectors worked in partnership for development.

In the long-term process of economic development, multilateral institutions, such as the United Nations and the World Bank, and the Western partners in African development (in Europe, North America, and elsewhere) can and should play a supportive role. But ultimately African development depends upon the African people. Just as Asians have turned economies that were seemingly basket cases into dynamic and even model developing countries, Africans face the challenge of putting into practice their own vision of development. It will inevitably take time and determination to make the economies grow, adjust, and develop. But with Africa's abundant natural and human resources, a more prosperous future is not out of reach.

Appendix

TABLE 1 Basic Indicators

	Population (millions) mid-1990	Area (thousand square km.)	GNP per capita: Dollars 1990	GNP per capita: Growth rate 1965–1990	Life expectancy 1990
Sub-Saharan Africa					
Mozambique	15.7	802	80	na	47
Tanzania	24.5	945	110	−0.2	48
Ethiopia	51.2	1,222	120	−0.2	48
Somalia	7.8	638	120	−0.1	48
Chad	5.7	1,284	190	−1.1	47
Malawi	8.5	118	200	0.9	46
Burundi	5.4	28	210	3.4	47
Zaire	37.3	2,345	220	−2.2	52
Uganda	16.3	236	220	−2.4	47
Madagascar	11.7	587	230	−1.9	51
Sierra Leone	4.1	72	240	0.0	42
Mali	8.5	1,240	270	1.7	48
Nigeria	115.5	924	290	0.1	52
Niger	7.7	1,267	310	−2.4	45
Rwanda	7.1	26	310	1.0	48
Burkina Faso	9.0	274	330	1.3	48
Benin	4.7	113	360	−0.1	50
Kenya	24.2	580	370	1.9	59
Ghana	14.9	239	390	−1.4	55
Central African Republic	3.0	623	390	−0.5	49
Togo	3.6	57	410	−0.1	54
Zambia	8.1	753	420	−1.9	50
Guinea	5.7	246	440	na	43
Mauritania	2.0	1,026	500	−0.6	47
Lesotho	1.8	30	530	4.9	56

(*continued*)

TABLE 1 Basic Indicators (Continued)

	Population (millions) mid-1990	Area (thousand square km.)	GNP per capita		Life expectancy 1990
			Dollars 1990	Growth rate 1965–1990	
Sub-Saharan Africa (continued)					
Liberia	2.6	111	na	na	54
Sudan	25.1	2,506	na	na	50
Zimbabwe	9.8	391	640	0.7	61
Senegal	7.4	197	710	−0.6	47
Côte d'Ivoire	11.9	322	750	0.5	55
Cameroon	11.7	475	960	3.0	57
Congo	2.3	342	1,010	3.1	53
Botswana	1.3	582	2,040	8.4	67
Mauritius	1.1	2	2,250	3.2	70
Angola	10.0	1,247	na	na	46
Namibia	1.8	824	na	na	57
Gabon	1.1	268	3,330	0.9	53
Other Africa					
Egypt	52.1	1,001	600	4.1	60
Morocco	25.1	447	950	2.3	62
Tunisia	8.1	164	1,440	3.2	67
Algeria	25.1	2,382	2,060	2.1	65
South Africa	35.9	1,221	2,530	1.3	62
Asia					
NIEs					
Hong Kong	5.8	1	11,490	6.2	78
Korea	42.8	99	5,400	7.1	71
Singapore	3.0	1	11,160	6.5	74
Taiwan	20.2	36	7,510[a]	na	na
ASEAN-4					
Indonesia	178.2	1,905	570	4.5	62
Malaysia	17.9	330	2,320	4.0	70
Philippines	61.5	300	730	1.3	64
Thailand	55.8	513	1,420	4.4	66
South Asia					
Bangladesh	106.7	144	210	0.7	52

(*continued*)

TABLE 1 Basic Indicators (Continued)

	Population (millions) mid-1990	Area (thousand square km.)	GNP per capita: Dollars 1990	GNP per capita: Growth rate 1965–1990	Life expectancy 1990
South Asia (continued)					
Myanmar	41.6	677	na	na	61
India	849.5	3,288	350	1.9	59
Nepal	18.9	141	170	0.5	52
Pakistan	112.4	796	380	2.5	56
Sri Lanka	17.0	66	470	2.9	71
China	1,133.7	9,561	370	5.8	70
Japan	123.5	378	25,430	4.1	79

NOTES: na = not available.
a. 1989.
SOURCES: World Bank 1992 and Asian Development Bank 1991.

TABLE 2 Growth of Production, 1965–1990, Average Annual Rate (Percentage)

	GDP		Agriculture		Manufacturing		Services, etc.	
	1965–80	1980–90	1965–80	1980–90	1965–80	1980–90	1965–80	1980–90
Sub-Saharan Africa								
Mozambique	na	−0.7	na	1.3	na	na	na	−3.2
Tanzania	3.9	2.8	1.6	4.1	5.6	−0.4	10.8	1.3
Ethiopia	2.7	1.8	1.2	−0.1	5.1	3.1	5.2	3.7
Somalia	3.5	2.4	na	3.3	na	−1.7	na	0.9
Chad	0.1	5.9	*−0.3*	2.7	*−0.6*	7.9	*0.2*	8.6
Malawi	5.5	2.9	*4.1*	2.0	na	3.6	*6.7*	3.5
Burundi	7.1	*3.9*	6.6	*3.1*	6.0	*5.5*	5.2	*5.4*
Zaire	1.9	1.8	na	2.5	na	2.3	na	1.6
Uganda	0.6	2.8	1.2	2.5	−3.7	5.2	1.1	3.3
Madagascar	1.6	1.1	na	2.4	na	na	na	0.3
Sierra Leone	2.7	1.5	3.9	2.6	0.7	−1.6	4.3	1.4
Mali	4.2	4.0	2.8	2.3	na	na	7.6	5.6
Nigeria	6.0	1.4	1.7	3.3	14.6	−1.0	5.9	2.7
Niger	0.3	−1.3	−3.4	na	na	na	0.6	na
Rwanda	4.9	1.0	na	−1.5	na	1.0	na	3.9
Burkina Faso	na	4.3	na	3.3	na	2.6	na	4.9
Benin	2.1	*2.8*	na	*3.6*	na	*5.8*	na	*1.8*
Kenya	6.8	4.2	5.0	3.3	10.5	4.9	7.2	4.9
Ghana	1.3	3.0	1.6	1.0	2.5	4.0	1.1	5.7
Central African Republic	2.8	1.5	2.1	2.7	na	na	2.9	0.0
Togo	4.3	1.6	1.9	5.4	na	0.7	4.7	−0.2
Zambia	2.0	0.8	2.2	3.7	5.3	3.5	1.8	*0.2*
Guinea	na	na	na	na	na	na	na	na
Mauritania	2.1	1.4	−2.0	0.7	na	na	6.5	0.8
Lesotho	6.8	3.1	na	−0.7	na	13.5	na	5.6
Liberia	na	na	na	na	na	na	na	na
Sudan	3.8	na	2.9	na	3.1	na	4.9	na
Zimbabwe	5.0	2.9	na	2.4	na	2.8	na	3.4
Senegal	2.3	3.0	1.4	3.1	4.5	4.8	1.9	2.9
Côte d'Ivoire	6.8	0.5	3.3	1.0	na	na	11.8	−0.1
Cameroon	5.1	2.3	4.2	1.6	7.0	10.2	4.8	2.1
Congo	6.2	3.6	3.1	3.6	na	6.8	4.7	2.3
Botswana	13.9	11.3	9.7	−4.0	13.5	5.3	11.5	11.9
Mauritius	5.2	6.0	na	2.6	na	10.8	na	5.1
Angola	na	na	na	*−0.5*	na	*−4.6*	na	na
Namibia	na	*0.4*	na	−1.0	na	*1.4*	na	*3.0*
Gabon	9.5	2.3	na	na	na	na	na	na
Other Africa								
Egypt	7.3	5.0	2.7	2.5	6.9	4.3	13.7	6.7
Morocco	5.7	4.0	2.4	6.4	na	3.8	7.1	4.1
Tunisia	6.5	3.6	5.5	2.3	9.9	6.0	6.4	4.5

(continued)

TABLE 2 Growth of Production, 1965–1990, Average Annual Rate (Percentage) (Continued)

	GDP		Agriculture		Manufacturing		Services, etc.	
	1965–80	1980–90	1965–80	1980–90	1965–80	1980–90	1965–80	1980–90
Other Africa (continued)								
Algeria	na	3.1	na	4.3	na	3.0	na	2.9
South Africa	3.7	1.3	*3.0*	2.6	5.6	−0.1	4.7	2.4
Asia								
NIEs								
Hong Kong	8.6	*7.1*	na	na	na	na	na	na
Korea	9.9	9.7	3.0	2.8	18.7	12.7	9.6	9.2
Singapore	10.0	6.4	2.8	−6.2	13.2	6.6	9.1	7.2
Taiwan[a]	9.7	8.5	1.8	1.5	12.8	8.2	9.0	9.7
ASEAN-4								
Indonesia	7.0	5.5	4.3	3.2	12.0	12.5	7.3	6.7
Malaysia	7.4	5.2	na	3.8	na	8.8	na	4.2
Philippines	5.7	0.9	3.9	1.0	6.8	0.1	5.0	2.6
Thailand	7.3	7.6	4.6	4.1	11.2	8.9	7.4	7.8
South Asia								
Bangladesh	1.7	4.3	0.6	2.6	2.8	2.8	3.6	5.8
Myanmar	na	na	na	na	na	na	na	na
India	3.6	5.3	2.5	3.1	4.5	7.1	4.4	6.5
Nepal	1.9	4.6	1.1	4.8	na	na	na	na
Pakistan	5.2	6.3	3.3	4.3	5.7	7.7	5.9	6.9
Sri Lanka	4.0	4.0	2.7	2.3	3.2	6.3	4.6	4.7
China	6.8	9.5	2.8	6.1	8.9	14.4	11.9	9.1
Japan	6.4	*4.1*	−0.6	*1.3*	7.8	*5.3*	6.8	*3.8*

NOTES: Figures in italics are for years other than those specified. Na = not available.
a. For Taiwan, figures are growth rates for valued added in the periods 1971–1980 and 1981–1990.
SOURCES: World Bank 1992 and Asian Development Bank 1991.

TABLE 3 Population Growth and Projections

	Annual growth of population (percentage)			Population (millions)		
	1965–80	1980–90	1989–2000	1990	2000	2025
Sub-Saharan Africa						
Mozambique	2.5	2.6	3.0	16	21	42
Tanzania	2.9	3.1	3.1	25	33	64
Ethiopia	2.7	3.1	3.4	51	71	156
Somalia	2.9	3.1	3.1	8	11	21
Chad	2.0	2.4	2.7	6	7	14
Malawi	2.9	3.4	3.4	9	12	24
Burundi	1.9	2.8	3.1	5	7	14
Zaire	3.1	3.2	3.0	37	50	89
Uganda	3.0	2.5	3.3	16	23	42
Madagascar	2.5	3.0	2.8	12	15	26
Sierra Leone	2.0	2.4	2.6	4	5	10
Mali	2.1	2.5	3.0	8	11	23
Nigeria	2.5	3.2	2.8	115	153	255
Niger	2.6	3.3	3.3	8	11	24
Rwanda	3.3	3.3	3.9	7	10	23
Burkina Faso	2.1	2.6	2.9	9	12	22
Benin	2.7	3.2	2.9	5	6	10
Kenya	3.6	3.8	3.5	24	34	64
Ghana	2.2	3.4	3.0	15	20	34
Central African Republic	1.8	2.7	2.5	3	4	6
Togo	3.0	3.5	3.2	4	5	9
Zambia	3.0	3.7	3.1	8	11	20
Guinea	1.5	2.5	2.8	6	8	15
Mauritania	2.4	2.4	2.8	2	3	5
Lesotho	2.3	2.7	2.6	2	2	4
Liberia	3.0	3.1	3.0	3	3	6
Sudan	3.0	2.7	2.8	25	33	55
Zimbabwe	3.1	3.4	2.4	10	12	18
Senegal	2.9	2.9	3.1	7	10	19
Côte d'Ivoire	4.1	3.8	3.5	12	17	31
Cameroon	2.7	3.0	2.9	12	16	28
Congo	2.8	3.4	3.3	2	3	6
Botswana	3.6	3.3	2.5	1	2	2

(*continued*)

TABLE 3 Population Growth and Projections (Continued)

	Annual growth of population (percent)			Population (millions)		
	1965–80	1980–90	1989–2000	1990	2000	2025
Sub-Saharan Africa (continued)						
Mauritius	1.6	1.0	0.9	1	1	1
Angola	2.8	2.6	3.0	10	13	27
Namibia	2.4	3.2	3.0	2	2	4
Gabon	3.6	3.6	2.8	1	1	3
Other Africa						
Egypt	2.1	2.4	1.8	52	62	86
Morocco	2.5	2.6	2.4	25	32	47
Tunisia	2.1	2.3	1.9	8	10	14
Algeria	3.1	3.0	2.8	25	33	52
South Africa	2.4	2.4	2.2	36	45	65
Asia						
NIEs						
Hong Kong	2.0	1.4	0.8	6	6	7
Korea	2.0	1.1	0.9	43	47	54
Singapore	1.6	2.2	1.2	3	3	4
Taiwan	na	1.9	na	20	na	na
ASEAN-4						
Indonesia	2.4	1.8	1.6	178	209	275
Malaysia	2.5	2.6	2.3	18	22	32
Philippines	2.8	2.4	1.8	61	74	101
Thailand	2.9	1.8	1.4	56	64	84
South Asia						
Bangladesh	2.6	2.3	1.8	107	128	176
Myanmar	2.3	2.1	2.0	42	51	70
India	2.3	2.1	1.7	850	1,006	1,348
Nepal	2.4	2.6	2.5	19	24	37
Pakistan	3.1	3.1	2.7	112	147	240
Sri Lanka	1.8	1.4	1.1	17	19	24
China	2.2	1.4	1.3	1,134	1,294	1,597
Japan	1.2	0.6	0.3	124	128	128

NOTE: na = not available.
SOURCES: World Bank 1992 and Asian Development Bank 1991.

TABLE 4 Agriculture, 1965–1990

	Proportion of GDP (%)		Growth rate %		Index of food (1979–81 = 100)
	1965	1990	1965–80	1980–90	1988–90
Sub-Saharan Africa					
Mozambique	na	65	na	1.3	81
Tanzania	46	59	1.6	4.1	88
Ethiopia	58	41	1.2	−0.1	84
Somalia	71	65	na	3.3	94
Chad	42	38	−0.3	2.7	85
Malawi	50	33	4.1	2.0	83
Burundi	na	56	6.6	3.1	92
Zaire	20	30	na	2.5	97
Uganda	52	67	1.2	2.5	95
Madagascar	25	33	na	2.4	88
Sierra Leone	34	32	3.9	2.6	89
Mali	65	46	2.8	2.3	97
Nigeria	55	36	1.7	3.3	106
Niger	68	36	−3.4	na	71
Rwanda	75	38	na	−1.5	77
Burkina Faso	37	32	na	3.3	114
Benin	59	37	na	3.6	112
Kenya	35	28	5.0	3.3	106
Ghana	44	48	1.6	1.0	97
Central African Republic	46	42	2.1	2.7	91
Togo	45	33	1.9	5.4	88
Zambia	14	17	2.2	3.7	103
Guinea	na	28	na	na	87
Mauritania	32	26	−2.0	0.7	85
Lesotho	65	24	na	−0.7	86
Liberia	27	na	na	na	84
Sudan	54	na	2.9	na	71
Zimbabwe	18	13	na	2.4	94
Senegal	25	21	1.4	3.1	102
Côte d'Ivoire	47	47	3.3	1.0	101
Cameroon	33	27	4.2	1.6	89
Congo	19	13	3.1	3.6	94

(*continued*)

TABLE 4 Agriculture, 1965–1990 (Continued)

	Proportion of GDP (%)		Growth rate %		Index of food (1979–81 = 100)
	1965	1990	1965–80	1980–90	1988–90
Sub-Saharan Africa (continued)					
Botswana	34	3	9.7	−4.0	75
Mauritius	16	12	na	2.6	100
Angola	na	13	na	−0.5	81
Namibia	na	11	na	−1.0	93
Gabon	26	9	na	na	84
Other Africa					
Egypt	29	17	2.7	2.5	118
Morocco	23	16	2.4	6.4	128
Tunisia	22	16	5.5	2.3	87
Algeria	na	13	na	4.3	96
South Africa	10	5	3.0	2.6	87
Asia					
NIEs					
Hong Kong	2	0	na	na	80
Korea	38	9	3.0	2.8	106
Singapore	3	0	2.8	−6.2	69
Taiwan[a]	17	4	1.8	1.5	na
ASEAN-4					
Indonesia	51	22	4.3	3.2	123
Malaysia	28	na	na	3.8	147
Philippines	26	22	3.9	1.0	84
Thailand	32	12	4.6	4.1	106
South Asia					
Bangladesh	53	38	0.6	2.6	96
Myanmar	na	na	na	na	93
India	44	31	2.5	3.1	119
Nepal	65	60	1.1	4.8	115
Pakistan	40	26	3.3	4.3	101
Sri Lanka	28	26	2.7	2.3	87
China	38	27	2.8	6.1	133
Japan	10	3	−0.6	1.3	101

NOTES: na = not available.

a. Figures for Taiwan are for 1970, 1990, 1971–1980, and 1981–1990, respectively.

SOURCES: World Bank 1992 and Asian Development Bank 1991.

TABLE 5 Health

	Population per physician (thousands)		Infant mortality rate (per 1,000 live births)		Daily calorie supply (per capita)	
	1965	1984	1965	1990	1965	1989
Sub-Saharan Africa						
Mozambique	18.0	na	179	137	1,712	1,680
Tanzania	21.7	25.0	138	115	1,831	2,206
Ethiopia	70.2	78.8	165	132	1,853	1,667
Somalia	43.8	20.0	165	126	1,718	1,906
Chad	72.5	38.4	183	125	2,395	1,743
Malawi	47.3	11.3	200	149	2,259	2,139
Burundi	55.9	21.0	142	107	2,131	1,932
Zaire	34.7	13.5	141	94	2,187	1,991
Uganda	11.1	na	119	117	2,361	2,153
Madagascar	10.6	9.8	201	116	2,447	2,158
Sierra Leone	16.8	13.6	208	147	2,014	1,799
Mali	51.5	25.4	207	166	1,938	2,314
Nigeria	29.5	6.4	162	98	2,185	2,312
Niger	65.5	39.7	180	128	1,996	2,308
Rwanda	72.5	35.1	141	120	1,856	1,971
Burkina Faso	74.0	57.2	190	134	1,882	2,288
Benin	32.4	15.9	166	113	2,019	2,305
Kenya	13.3	10.1	112	67	2,208	2,163
Ghana	13.7	20.4	120	85	1,937	2,248
Central African Republic	34.0	na	157	101	2,055	2,036
Togo	23.2	8.7	153	88	2,454	2,214
Zambia	11.4	7.2	121	82	2,072	2,077
Guinea	47.1	na	191	138	2,187	2,132
Mauritania	36.5	11.9	178	121	1,903	2,685
Lesotho	20.1	18.6	142	93	2,049	2,299
Liberia	12.6	9.3	176	136	2,158	2,382
Sudan	23.5	10.2	160	102	1,938	1,974
Zimbabwe	8.0	6.7	103	49	2,075	2,299
Senegal	19.5	na	160	81	2,372	2,369
Côe d'Ivoire	20.6	na	149	95	2,352	2,577
Cameroon	26.7	na	143	88	2,011	2,217
Congo	14.2	na	129	116	2,260	2,590

(*continued*)

TABLE 5 Health (Continued)

	Population per physician (thousands)		Infant mortality rate (per 1,000 live births)		Daily calorie supply (per capita)	
	1965	1984	1965	1990	1965	1989
Sub-Saharan Africa (continued)						
Botswana	27.5	6.9	112	38	2,045	2,375
Mauritius	3.9	1.9	65	20	2,269	2,887
Angola	13.2	17.8	192	130	1,907	1,807
Namibia	na	na	145	100	1,900	1,946
Gabon	na	2.8	153	97	1,950	2,383
Other Africa						
Egypt	2.3	0.8	145	66	2,399	3,336
Morocco	12.1	4.7	145	67	2,112	3,020
Tunisia	8.0	2.2	145	44	2,217	3,121
Algeria	8.6	2.3	154	67	1,701	2,866
South Africa	2.1	na	124	66	2,759	3,122
Asia						
NIEs						
Hong Kong	2.5	1.1	27	7	2,486	2,853
Korea	2.7	1.2	62	17	2,178	2,852
Singapore	1.9	1.4	26	7	2,285	3,198
Taiwan	na	na	na	na	na	na
ASEAN-4						
Indonesia	31.7	9.4	128	61	1,791	2,750
Malaysia	6.2	1.9	55	16	2,353	2,774
Philippines	na	6.6	72	41	1,875	2,375
Thailand	7.2	6.3	88	27	2,138	2,316
South Asia						
Bangladesh	8.1	6.4	144	105	1,970	2,021
Myanmar	11.9	3.7	122	64	1,897	2,440
India	4.9	2.5	150	92	2,021	2,229
Nepal	46.2	30.2	171	121	1,889	2,077
Pakistan	na	2.9	149	103	1,773	2,219
Sri Lanka	5.8	5.5	63	19	2,171	2,277
China	1.6	1.0	90	29	1,929	2,639
Japan	1.0	0.7	18	5	2,668	2,956

NOTE: na = not available.

SOURCE: "World Development Indicators," World Bank 1992.

TABLE 6 Education

	Percentage of age group enrolled in education						Adult illiteracy (percentage)
	Primary		Secondary		Tertiary		
	1965	1989	1965	1989	1965	1989	1990
Sub-Saharan Africa							
Mozambique	37	68	3	5	0	0	67
Tanzania	32	63	2	4	0	0	na
Ethiopia	11	38	2	15	0	1	na
Somalia	10	na	2	na	0	na	76
Chad	34	57	1	7	na	1	70
Malawi	44	67	2	4	0	1	na
Burundi	26	71	1	4	0	1	50
Zaire	70	78	5	24	0	2	28
Uganda	67	77	4	13	0	1	52
Madagascar	65	92	8	19	1	4	20
Sierra Leone	29	53	5	18	0	1	79
Mali	24	23	4	6	0	na	68
Nigeria	32	70	5	19	0	3	49
Niger	11	28	1	6	na	1	72
Rwanda	53	69	2	7	0	1	50
Burkina Faso	12	35	1	7	0	1	82
Benin	34	65	3	na	0	2	77
Kenya	54	94	4	23	0	2	31
Ghana	69	75	13	39	1	2	40
Central African Republic	56	64	2	11	na	1	62
Togo	55	103	5	22	0	3	57
Zambia	53	95	7	20	na	2	27
Guinea	31	34	5	9	0	1	76
Mauritania	13	51	1	16	na	3	66
Lesotho	94	110	4	26	0	4	na
Liberia	41	na	5	na	1	3	61
Sudan	29	na	4	na	1	3	73
Zimbabwe	110	125	6	52	0	6	33
Senegal	40	58	7	16	1	3	62
Côte d'Ivoire	60	na	6	20	0	na	46
Cameroon	94	101	5	26	0	3	46
Congo	114	na	10	na	1	6	43

(continued)

TABLE 6 Education (Continued)

	Percentage of age group enrolled in education						Adult illiteracy (percentage)
	Primary		Secondary		Tertiary		
	1965	1989	1965	1989	1965	1989	1990
Sub-Saharan Africa (continued)							
Botswana	65	111	3	37	na	3	26
Mauritius	101	103	26	53	3	2	na
Angola	39	94	5	11	0	na	58
Namibia	na	na	na	na	na	na	na
Gabon	134	na	11	na	na	4	39
Other Africa							
Egypt	75	97	26	81	7	20	52
Morocco	57	68	11	36	1	11	51
Tunisia	91	115	16	44	2	8	35
Algeria	68	94	7	61	1	11	43
South Africa	90	na	15	na	4	na	na
Asia							
NIEs							
Hong Kong	103	105	29	73	5	na	na
Korea	101	108	35	86	6	38	na
Singapore	105	110	45	69	10	na	na
Taiwan	na	na	na	na	na	na	na
ASEAN-4							
Indonesia	72	118	12	47	1	na	23
Malaysia	90	96	28	59	2	7	22
Philippines	113	111	41	73	19	28	10
Thailand	78	86	14	28	2	16	7
South Asia							
Bangladesh	49	70	13	17	1	4	65
Myanmar	71	103	15	24	1	5	19
India	74	98	27	43	5	na	52
Nepal	20	86	5	30	1	6	74
Pakistan	40	38	12	20	2	5	65
Sri Lanka	93	107	35	74	2	4	12
China	89	135	24	44	0	2	27
Japan	100	102	82	96	13	31	na

NOTE: na = not available.
SOURCE: "World Development Indicators," World Bank 1992.

TABLE 7 Savings and Investment, 1965–1990, Percentage of GDP

	Gross domestic savings		Gross domestic investment	
	1965	1990	1965	1990
Sub-Saharan Africa				
Mozambique	na	−12	na	37
Tanzania	16	−6	15	25
Ethiopia	12	6	13	13
Somalia	8	22	11	16
Chad	6	−15	12	10
Malawi	0	10	14	19
Burundi	4	1	6	19
Zaire	16	na	17	11
Uganda	12	−1	11	12
Madagascar	0	8	7	17
Sierra Leone	8	5	12	11
Mali	5	10	18	26
Nigeria	10	29	15	15
Niger	3	na	8	9
Rwanda	5	4	10	12
Burkina Faso	4	5	10	20
Benin	3	2	11	12
Kenya	15	18	14	24
Ghana	8	11	18	15
Central African Republic	11	−2	21	11
Togo	23	11	22	22
Zambia	40	17	25	14
Guinea	na	21	na	20
Mauritania	27	3	14	15
Lesotho	−26	−41	11	71
Liberia	27	na	17	na
Sudan	9	na	10	na
Zimbabwe	23	21	15	21
Senegal	8	9	12	13
Côte d'Ivoire	29	14	22	10
Cameroon	12	19	13	17
Congo	5	31	22	16
Botswana	−13	na	6	na

(*continued*)

TABLE 7 Savings and Investment, 1965–1990, Percentage of GDP (Continued)

	Gross domestic savings		Gross domestic investment	
	1965	1990	1965	1990
Sub-Saharan Africa (continued)				
Mauritius	13	21	17	30
Angola	na	na	na	na
Namibia	na	na	na	na
Gabon	37	37	31	19
Other Africa				
Egypt	14	10	18	23
Morocco	12	20	10	26
Tunisia	14	19	28	27
Algeria	19	38	22	33
South Africa	26	25	27	19
Asia				
NIEs				
Hong Kong	29	33	36	28
Korea	8	37	15	37
Singapore	10	45	22	39
Taiwan	na	28	na	22
ASEAN-4				
Indonesia	8	37	8	36
Malaysia	24	33	20	34
Philippines	21	16	21	22
Thailand	19	34	20	37
South Asia				
Bangladesh	8	2	11	12
Myanmar	na	na	na	na
India	15	20	17	23
Nepal	0	8	6	18
Pakistan	13	12	21	19
Sri Lanka	13	15	12	22
China	25	43	24	39
Japan	33	34	32	33

NOTE: na = not available.
SOURCES: World Bank 1992 and Asian Development Bank 1991.

TABLE 8 Official Development Assistance, 1988–1990

	Millions of dollars			Per capita (dollars)	As a % of GNP
	1988	1989	1990	1990	1990
Sub-Saharan Africa					
Mozambique	893	772	946	60.2	65.7
Tanzania	982	920	1,155	47.1	48.2
Ethiopia	970	752	888	17.4	14.6
Somalia	433	427	428	54.8	45.9
Chad	264	241	315	55.5	28.6
Malawi	366	412	479	56.3	25.7
Burundi	188	196	265	48.8	24.0
Zaire	576	634	823	22.0	10.9
Uganda	363	403	557	34.1	18.4
Madagascar	304	321	382	32.8	12.3
Sierra Leone	102	100	70	16.9	7.8
Mali	427	454	474	56.0	19.4
Nigeria	120	346	234	2.0	0.7
Niger	371	296	358	46.7	14.2
Rwanda	252	232	287	40.3	13.4
Burkina Faso	298	272	315	34.9	9.9
Benin	162	263	261	55.1	na
Kenya	808	967	1,000	41.4	11.4
Ghana	474	552	465	31.2	7.4
Central African Republic	196	192	232	76.3	17.8
Togo	199	183	210	57.8	13.0
Zambia	478	392	438	54.0	14.0
Guinea	262	346	292	51.0	10.4
Mauritania	184	242	211	107.0	20.0
Lesotho	108	127	138	78.0	24.5
Liberia	65	59	115	44.9	na
Sudan	937	772	792	31.5	9.3
Zimbabwe	273	265	343	35.0	5.5
Senegal	569	650	739	99.8	12.7
Côte d'Ivoire	439	403	689	57.9	6.9
Cameroon	284	458	483	41.2	4.3
Congo	89	91	209	92.0	7.3

(*continued*)

TABLE 8 Official Development Assistance, 1988–1990 (Continued)

	Millions of dollars 1988	1989	1990	Per capita (dollars) 1990	As a % of GNP 1990
Sub-Saharan Africa (continued)					
Botswana	151	160	148	118.2	5.5
Mauritius	59	58	89	82.9	3.6
Angola	159	148	212	21.2	na
Namibia	22	59	57	32.0	na
Gabon	106	133	140	123.0	3.0
Other Africa					
Egypt	1,537	1,568	5,604	107.6	15.9
Morocco	481	450	970	38.6	3.8
Tunisia	316	234	316	39.2	2.5
Algeria	171	152	227	9.1	0.4
South Africa	na	na	na	na	na
Asia					
NIEs					
Hong Kong	22	40	37	6.4	0.1
Korea	10	52	52	1.2	0.0
Singapore	22	95	−3	−1.0	0.0
Taiwan	na	na	na	na	na
ASEAN-4					
Indonesia	1,632	1,839	1,724	9.7	1.6
Malaysia	104	140	469	26.3	1.1
Philippines	854	844	1,277	20.8	2.9
Thailand	563	739	805	14.4	1.0
South Asia					
Bangladesh	1,592	1,800	2,103	19.7	9.2
Myanmar	451	184	170	4.1	0.8
India	2,097	1,895	1,586	1.9	0.6
Nepal	399	493	429	22.7	13.8
Pakistan	1,408	1,129	1,152	10.3	2.9
Sri Lanka	598	547	665	39.1	8.2
China	1,989	2,153	2,076	1.8	0.6
Japan	na	na	na	na	na

NOTE: na = not available.

SOURCE: "World Development Indicators," World Bank 1992.

TABLE 9 Total External Debt, 1990

	Millions of dollars	Debt/GNP ratio	Debt service (% of exports)
Sub-Saharan Africa			
Mozambique	4,718	3.8	14.4
Tanzania	5,866	2.8	25.8
Ethiopia	3,250	0.5	33.0
Somalia	2,350	2.8	11.7
Chad	492	0.5	5.1
Malawi	1,544	0.9	22.5
Burundi	906	0.8	43.6
Zaire	10,115	1.4	15.4
Uganda	2,726	0.9	54.5
Madagascar	3,938	1.3	47.2
Sierra Leone	1,189	1.5	15.9
Mali	2,433	1.0	11.5
Nigeria	36,068	1.1	20.3
Niger	1,829	0.7	24.1
Rwanda	741	0.4	14.5
Burkina Faso	834	0.3	6.4
Benin	1,427	na	3.4
Kenya	6,840	0.8	33.8
Ghana	3,498	0.6	34.9
Central African Republic	901	0.7	11.9
Togo	1,296	0.8	14.1
Zambia	7,223	2.6	12.3
Guinea	2,497	1.0	8.3
Mauritania	2,227	2.3	13.9
Lesotho	390	0.4	2.4
Liberia	1,870	na	na
Sudan	15,383	na	5.8
Zimbabwe	3,199	0.5	22.6
Senegal	3,745	0.7	20.4
Côte d'Ivoire	17,956	2.0	38.6
Cameroon	6,023	0.6	21.5
Congo	5,118	2.0	20.7
Botswana	516	0.2	4.4
Mauriitius	939	0.4	8.7
Angola	7,710	na	na

(*continued*)

TABLE 9 Total External Debt, 1990 (Continued)

	Millions of dollars	Debt/GNP ratio	Debt service (% of exports)
Sub-Saharan Africa (continued)			
Namibia	na	na	na
Gabon	3,647	0.9	7.6
Other Africa			
Egypt	39,885	1.3	25.7
Morocco	23,524	1.0	23.4
Tunisia	7,534	0.6	25.8
Algeria	26,806	0.5	59.4
South Africa	na	na	na
Asia			
NIEs			
Hong Kong	na	na	na
Korea	34,014	0.1	10.7
Singapore	na	na	na
Taiwan	881	na	na
ASEAN-4			
Indonesia	67,908	0.7	30.9
Malaysia	19,502	0.5	11.7
Philippines	30,456	0.7	21.2
Thailand	25,868	0.3	17.2
South Asia			
Bangladesh	12,245	0.5	25.4
Myanmar	4,675	na	na
India	70,115	0.2	28.8
Nepal	1,621	0.5	18.2
Pakistan	20,683	0.5	22.8
Sri Lanka	5,851	0.7	13.8
China	52,555	0.1	10.3
Japan	na	na	na

NOTE: na = not available.
SOURCES: World Bank 1992 and Asian Development Bank 1991.

TABLE 10 Growth of Merchandise Trade, 1965–1990

	Merchandise trade (millions of dollars)		Average annual growth rate (percentage)				Terms of trade (1987 = 100)	
	Exports	Imports	Exports		Imports			
	1990	1990	1965–80	1980–90	1965–80	1980–90	1985	1990
Sub-Saharan Africa								
Mozambique	na	na	na	na	na	na	na	na
Tanzania	300	935	−4	−7	2	−1	101	108
Ethiopia	297	1,081	−1	0	−1	4	117	84
Somalia	130	360	4	−3	4	−4	107	111
Chad	200	450	na	na	na	na	na	na
Malawi	412	576	5	4	3	1	104	93
Burundi	75	235	3	−2	0	5	133	70
Zaire	999	888	5	−11	−3	−4	111	163
Uganda	151	458	−3	−2	−5	3	143	88
Madagascar	335	480	1	−2	0	0	98	102
Sierra Leone	138	146	−2	−1	−5	−2	106	80
Mali	347	640	10	10	4	7	95	97
Nigeria	13,671	5,688	11	−2	15	−15	167	100
Niger	435	230	13	4	7	−9	126	77
Rwanda	112	279	8	0	5	11	116	98
Burkina Faso	160	480	4	10	6	1	108	100
Benin	93	483	na	na	na	na	na	na
Kenya	1,033	2,124	4	1	2	2	114	103
Ghana	739	1,199	−3	4	−1	0	106	75
Central African Republic	130	170	−1	−1	−5	6	107	109
Togo	300	700	6	2	9	1	118	114
Zambia	na	na	na	na	na	na	na	na
Guinea	na	na	na	na	na	na	na	na
Mauritania	468	248	4	4	6	−5	113	107
Lesotho	na	na	na	na	na	na	na	na
Liberia	500	450	4	−3	2	−2	97	111
Sudan	400	600	0	−1	2	−8	106	100
Zimbabwe	na	1,851	na	na	na	na	100	na
Senegal	783	1,620	3	6	4	5	106	106
Côte d'Ivoire	2,600	2,100	6	3	8	−1	110	80
Cameroon	1,200	1,300	5	−1	6	−3	139	91
Congo	1,130	570	10	6	1	−3	145	99
Botswana	na	na	na	na	na	na	na	na
Mauritius	1,182	1,616	3	10	5	11	83	114
Angola	3,000	1,200	na	na	na	na	na	na
Namibia	na	na	na	na	na	na	na	na
Gabon	2,471	760	9	1	10	−2	140	96

(*continued*)

TABLE 10 Growth of Merchandise Trade, 1965–1990 (Continued)

	Merchandise trade (millions of dollars)		Average annual growth rate (percentage)				Terms of trade (1987 = 100)	
	Exports	Imports	Exports		Imports			
	1990	1990	1965–80	1980–90	1965–80	1980–90	1985	1990
Other Africa								
Egypt	2,985	10,340	0	2	4	−2	131	76
Morocco	4,263	6,918	4	6	7	3	88	86
Tunisia	3,498	5,471	11	5	10	1	105	99
Algeria	15,241	10,433	2	5	13	−5	174	99
South Africa	23,612	18,258	8	2	0	−4	105	93
Asia								
NIEs								
Hong Kong	29,002	82,495	9	6	8	11	97	100
Korea	64,837	69,585	27	13	15	11	103	108
Singapore	52,627	60,647	5	9	7	7	99	100
Taiwan	66,240	52,700	na	15[a]	na	18[a]	na	na
ASEAN-4								
Indonesia	25,553	21,837	10	3	13	1	134	111
Malaysia	29,409	29,251	5	10	2	6	117	94
Philippines	8,681	13,080	5	3	3	2	93	93
Thailand	23,002	33,129	9	13	4	10	91	99
South Asia								
Bangladesh	1,674	3,646	na	8	na	8	109	95
Myanmar	322	270	−2	−10	−4	−15	106	127
India	17,967	23,692	3	7	1	4	96	96
Nepal	162	543	na	na	na	na	98	na
Pakistan	5,590	7,377	−2	9	0	4	90	95
Sri Lanka	1,984	2,689	0	7	−1	2	103	90
China	62,091	53,345	5	11	7	10	109	111
Japan	286,768	231,223	11	4	5	6	71	91

NOTES: na = not available.
a. 1985–1990.
SOURCES: World Bank 1992 and Asian Development Bank 1991.

TABLE 11 Macroeconomic Stability, 1965–1990

	GNP per capita growth rate (percentage) 1965–1990	Average annual rate of inflation (percentage)	
		1965–1980	1980–1990
Sub-Saharan Africa			
Mozambique	na	na	36.6
Tanzania	−0.2	9.6	25.8
Ethiopia	−0.2	3.4	2.1
Somalia	−0.1	10.2	49.7
Chad	−1.1	6.2	1.2
Malawi	0.9	7.4	14.7
Burundi	3.4	5.0	4.2
Zaire	−2.2	24.7	60.9
Uganda	−2.4	21.4	107.0
Madagascar	−1.9	7.7	17.1
Sierra Leone	0.0	7.9	56.1
Mali	1.7	9.0	3.0
Nigeria	0.1	14.6	17.7
Niger	−2.4	7.5	2.9
Rwanda	1.0	12.5	3.8
Burkina Faso	1.3	6.3	4.5
Benin	−0.1	7.4	1.9
Kenya	1.9	7.2	9.2
Ghana	−1.4	22.9	42.5
Central African Republic	−0.5	8.2	5.4
Togo	−0.1	7.1	4.8
Zambia	−1.9	6.3	42.2
Guinea	na	na	na
Mauritania	−0.6	7.6	9.0
Lesotho	4.9	6.7	12.7
Liberia	na	6.3	na
Sudan	na	11.5	na
Zimbabwe	0.7	5.8	10.8
Senegal	−0.6	6.3	6.7
Côte d'Ivoire	0.5	9.4	2.3
Cameroon	3.0	9.0	5.6
Congo	3.1	6.8	0.5

(*continued*)

TABLE 11 Macroeconomic Stability, 1965–1990 (Continued)

	GNP per capita growth rate (percentage) 1965–1990	Average annual rate of inflation (percentage)	
		1965–1980	1980–1990
Sub-Saharan Africa (continued)			
Botswana	8.4	8.4	12.0
Mauritius	3.2	11.8	8.8
Angola	na	na	na
Namibia	na	na	13.4
Gabon	0.9	12.8	−1.7
Other Africa			
Egypt	4.1	6.4	11.8
Morocco	2.3	7.0	7.2
Tunisia	3.2	6.7	7.4
Algeria	2.1	10.9	6.6
South Africa	1.3	10.3	14.4
Asia			
NIEs			
Hong Kong	6.2	8.1	7.2
Korea	7.1	18.4	5.1
Singapore	6.5	5.1	1.7
Taiwan[a]	9.1	11.1	3.1
ASEAN-4			
Indonesia	4.5	35.5	8.4
Malaysia	4.0	4.9	1.6
Philippines	1.3	11.4	14.9
Thailand	4.4	6.2	3.4
South Asia			
Bangladesh	0.7	15.9	9.6
Myanmar	na	na	na
India	1.9	7.5	7.9
Nepal	0.5	7.8	9.1
Pakistan	2.5	10.3	6.7
Sri Lanka	2.9	9.4	11.1
China	5.8	−0.3	5.8
Japan	4.1	7.7	1.5

NOTES: na = not available.
a. Figures for Taiwan are for 1971–1990, 1971–1980, and 1981–1990, respectively.
SOURCES: World Bank 1992 and Asian Development Bank 1991.

TABLE 12 Central Government Current Revenue, 1972–1990

	Percentage of total current revenue							
	Direct taxes		Domestic transactions taxes		International transactions taxes		Total current revenue as a % of GNP	
	1972	1990	1972	1990	1972	1990	1972	1990
Sub-Saharan Africa								
Mozambique	na	na	na	na	na	na	na	na
Tanzania	29.9	na	29.1	na	21.7	na	15.8	na
Ethiopia	23.0	na	29.8	na	30.4	na	10.5	na
Somalia	10.7	na	24.7	na	45.3	na	13.7	na
Chad	16.7	na	12.3	na	45.2	na	10.8	na
Malawi	31.4	35	24.2	33.2	20.0	17.7	16	23.7
Burundi	18.1	na	18.3	na	40.3	na	11.5	na
Zaire	22.5	28.9	12.1	16.5	57.8	47.3	10.2	12.0
Uganda	22.1	5.5	32.8	19.1	36.3	75.3	13.7	5.3
Madagascar	13.1	na	29.9	na	33.6	na	14.7	na
Sierra Leone	32.7	26.3	14.6	25.7	42.4	44.6	19.5	8.8
Mali	na	10.8	na	28.6	na	12.0	na	18.9
Nigeria	43.0	na	26.3	na	17.5	na	10.3	na
Niger	na	na	na	na	na	na	na	na
Rwanda	17.9	na	14.1	na	41.7	na	9.8	na
Burkina Faso	16.8	na	18.0	na	51.8	na	8.6	na
Benin	na	na	na	na	na	na	na	na
Kenya	35.6	27.4	19.9	42.8	24.3	15.8	18.0	22.6
Ghana	18.4	28.7	29.4	28.3	40.6	35.2	15.1	13.9
Central African Republic	na	23.9	na	13.1	na	45.2	na	13.3
Togo	na	na	na	na	na	na	na	na
Zambia	49.7	38.1	20.2	37.0	14.3	15.8	23.2	11.9
Guinea	na	na	na	17.1	na	74.4	na	14.6
Mauritania	na	32.3	na	19.4	na	36.8	na	21.8
Lesotho	14.3	12.4	2.0	22.8	62.9	54.5	11.7	21.2
Liberia	40.4	33.9	20.3	25.1	31.6	34.6	17.0	17.8
Sudan	11.8	na	30.4	na	40.5	na	18	na
Zimbabwe	na	44.9	na	26.3	na	17.5	na	35.6
Senegal	17.5	na	24.5	na	30.9	na	16.9	na
Côte d'Ivoire	na	na	na	na	na	na	na	na
Cameroon	na	45.2	na	20.2	na	14.0	na	17.7
Congo	19.4	na	40.3	na	26.5	na	18.4	na

(*continued*)

TABLE 12 Central Government Current Revenue, 1972–1990 (Continued)

	Percentage of total current revenue							
	Direct taxes		Domestic transactions taxes		International transactions taxes		Total current revenue as a % of GNP	
	1972	1990	1972	1990	1972	1990	1972	1990
Sub-Saharan Africa (continued)								
Botswana	20.1	38.6	1.4	1.5	47.7	13.2	30.4	60.9
Mauritius	22.7	13.9	23.3	20.9	40.2	46.4	15.6	24.2
Angola	na	na	na	na	na	na	na	na
Namibia	na	42.7	na	28.5	na	16.4	na	43.6
Gabon	18.2	na	9.5	na	44.9	na	26.1	na
Other Africa								
Egypt	na	15.9	na	11.9	na	14.0	na	35.9
Morocco	16.4	na	45.7	na	13.2	na	18.5	na
Tunisia	15.9	12.9	31.6	20.1	21.8	27.9	23.6	31.8
Algeria	na	na	na	na	na	na	na	na
South Africa	54.8	48.6	21.5	34.1	4.6	4.9	22.1	30.9
Asia								
NIEs								
Hong Kong	na	na	na	na	na	na	na	na
Korea	29.0	34.0	41.7	33.5	10.7	10.6	13.1	15.7
Singapore	24.4	24.3	17.6	19.6	11.1	2.5	21.5	27.9
Taiwan	na	na	na	na	na	na	na	13.3
ASEAN-4								
Indonesia	45.5	57.5	22.8	25.1	17.6	6.0	13.4	18.3
Malaysia	25.2	30.5	24.2	24.3	27.9	16.7	20.3	28.9
Philippines	13.8	28.3	24.3	30.7	23.0	25.1	13.1	16.3
Thailand	12.1	24.2	46.3	41.4	28.7	22.1	12.5	19.9
South Asia								
Bangladesh	3.7	8.6	22.4	25.8	18.0	27.3	8.4	11.4
Myanmar	28.7	9.0	34.2	30.7	13.4	14.9	na	na
India	21.3	15.4	44.5	35.5	20.1	28.8	10.2	14.8
Nepal	4.1	10.8	26.4	35.7	36.7	31.0	5.2	10.0
Pakistan	13.6	10.0	35.9	32.2	34.2	30.6	12.5	19.0
Sri Lanka	19.1	10.8	34.7	46.4	35.4	28.6	20.1	21.1
China	na	na	na	na	na	na	na	na
Japan	64.8	71.2	22.6	12.0	3.5	1.3	11.2	13.9

NOTE: na = not available.
SOURCES: World Bank 1992 and Asian Development Bank 1991.

TABLE 13 Central Government Expenditure, 1972–1990

	Defense (percentage of total expenditure)		Education and health (percentage of total expenditure)		Expenditure as a percentage of GNP		Surplus/deficit as a percentage of GNP	
	1972	1990	1972	1990	1972	1990	1972	1990
Sub-Saharan Africa								
Mozambique	na	na	na	na	na	na	na	na
Tanzania	11.9	na	24.5	na	19.7	na	−5.0	na
Ethiopia	14.3	na	20.1	na	13.7	na	−1.4	na
Somalia	23.3	na	12.7	na	13.5	na	0.6	na
Chad	24.6	na	19.2	na	14.9	na	−2.7	na
Malawi	3.1	5.4	21.3	16.2	22.1	29.2	−6.2	−1.9
Burundi	10.3	na	29.4	na	19.9	na	0.0	na
Zaire	11.1	6.7	17.5	2.1	14.1	13.0	−2.7	1.9
Uganda	23.1	na	20.6	na	21.8	na	−8.1	na
Madagascar	3.6	na	13.3	na	16.7	na	−2.0	na
Sierra Leone	3.6	5.3	20.8	14.0	23.9	11.1	−4.4	−1.4
Mali	na	8.0	na	11.1	na	28.9	na	−4.6
Nigeria	40.2	na	8.1	na	9.1	na	−0.8	na
Niger	na	na	na	na	na	na	na	na
Rwanda	25.6	na	27.9	na	12.5	na	−2.7	na
Burkina Faso	11.5	na	28.8	na	8.4	na	0.3	na
Benin	na	na	na	na	na	na	na	na
Kenya	6.0	7.8	29.8	25.2	21.0	31.4	−3.9	−6.8
Ghana	7.9	3.2	26.4	34.7	19.5	14.0	−5.8	0.4
Central African Republic	na	na	na	na	na	26.1	na	na
Togo	na	na	na	na	na	na	na	na
Zambia	0.0	0.0	26.4	16.0	34.0	21.9	−13.8	−5.0
Guinea	na	na	na	na	na	24.9	na	−4.2
Mauritania	na	na	na	na	na	33.5	na	−4.2
Lesotho	0.0	9.9	27.5	22.6	16.6	25.1	−0.9	−2.8
Liberia	5.3	9.8	25.0	17.0	16.7	na	1.1	na
Sudan	24.1	na	14.7	na	19.2	na	−0.8	na
Zimbabwe	na	16.5	na	31.0	na	40.5	na	−7.9
Senegal	na	na	na	na	17.4	na	−0.8	na
Côte d'Ivoire	na	na	na	na	na	na	na	na
Cameroon	na	6.7	na	15.4	na	20.8	na	−3.2
Congo	na	na	na	na	na	na	na	na

(*continued*)

TABLE 13 Central Government Expenditure, 1972–1990 (Continued)

	Defense (percentage of total expenditure)		Education and health (percentage of total expenditure)		Expenditure as a percentage of GNP		Surplus/deficit as a percentage of GNP	
	1972	1990	1972	1990	1972	1990	1972	1990
Sub-Saharan Africa (continued)								
Botswana	0.0	11.6	16.0	25.0	33.7	42.2	−23.8	12.6
Mauritius	0.8	1.3	23.8	23.0	16.3	24.2	−1.2	−0.5
Angola	na	na	na	na	na	na	na	na
Namibia	na	5.5	na	31.9	na	42.8	na	7.0
Gabon	na	na	na	na	37.0	na	−11.9	na
Other Africa								
Egypt	na	12.7	na	16.2	na	40.2	na	−6.9
Morocco	12.3	na	24.0	na	22.8	na	−3.9	na
Tunisia	4.9	6.5	37.9	22.4	23.1	37.2	−0.9	−4.5
Algeria	na	na	na	na	na	na	na	na
South Africa	na	na	na	na	22.7	34.6	−4.4	−2.5
Asia								
NIEs								
Hong Kong	na	na	na	na	na	na	na	na
Korea	25.8	25.8	17.0	21.8	18.0	15.7	−3.9	−0.7
Singapore	35.3	21.6	23.5	22.8	16.7	23.3	1.3	10.5
Taiwan	na	na	na	na	na	15.0	na	1.6
ASEAN-4								
Indonesia	18.6	8.0	8.8	10.4	15.1	20.4	−2.5	−2.1
Malaysia	na	na	na	na	26.5	31.3	−9.4	−2.8
Philippines	10.9	11.0	19.5	21.0	14.2	19.8	−2.1	−3.5
Thailand	20.2	17.3	23.6	26.9	16.7	15.1	−4.2	4.9
South Asia								
Bangladesh	5.1	10.1	19.8	16.0	9.2	15.0	−1.9	−0.4
Myanmar	31.6	24.7	21.1	21.4	na	na	na	na
India	26.2	17.0	3.8	4.1	10.5	18.2	−3.2	−7.3
Nepal	7.2	6.0	11.9	15.7	8.5	20.4	−1.2	−8.1
Pakistan	39.9	30.9	2.3	2.7	16.9	23.6	−6.9	−7.2
Sri Lanka	3.1	7.4	19.4	15.3	25.4	28.4	−5.3	−7.9
China	na	na	na	na	na	na	na	na
Japan	na	na	na	na	12.7	16.7	−1.9	−2.9

NOTE: na = not available.

SOURCES: World Bank 1992 and Asian Development Bank 1991.

NOTES

1. For a thorough and balanced study of the impact of population growth on economic development, see Johnson and Lee et al. 1986. For example, they feel that the reduction in fertility in China had a positive effect on per capita agricultural income, but that the agricultural policy reforms begun in 1979 were more important. While noting that some problems and inefficiencies in Africa may be due to the sparseness of population, the authors state (p. 89) that in contrast to China, "Tropical Africa has a comparatively high land/population ratio, but appears to be particularly vulnerable to problems induced by population growth."

2. The tiny country of Comoros (with a population of half a million) actually registered the highest increase.

3. One must add that studies of international purchasing power conclude that China's exchange rate is extremely undervalued, and thus standard comparisons of per capita income in dollar terms understate China's level of development, perhaps by as much as a factor of four (Summers and Heston 1991). Yet a correction of income measures for purchasing power parity does not alter the basic conclusions of either the cited report or this paper—that Asian countries devote more public and private resources to HRD relative to their incomes, while African countries seem to devote less, with less effect, than their more successful Asian counterparts.

4. While this general conclusion holds across countries and regions, it is disturbing that estimates for Africa are much lower in absolute terms, indicating major differences in the quality of basic education in the two regions (Glewwe 1991). Improvements in the quality of education would raise the private rate of return to investments in schooling.

5. Although some nominal "one-stop investment" offices have been set up in African countries, in many cases further streamlining is necessary to prevent them from being merely "a tissue-paper overlay of additional obfuscation and graft" (African businessman quoted by Laura Bailey, personal communication, July 1993).

6. As Laura Bailey notes, "The lump-sum tax is one of the most commonly enforced and collected taxes in Francophone Africa, but the actual amount levied is almost always a negotiated sum and an estimated 70% gets skimmed off before any deposits are made to the government" (personal communication, July 1993).

7. Obviously, employment creation per se may not be a sign of economic health. Robert C. Young (1992) distinguishes between "soft" and "hard" employment; "soft" employment refers to new jobs with very low-income jobs created as a result

of unemployment or underemployment, whereas "hard" employment refers to high productivity jobs created by innovations and new technologies. "Expansion of employment in the 'soft' sector is often not a sign of economic health but of stagnation" (p. 6).

8. For a more thorough treatment of this subject, see Bruton 1992.

9. For example, "field work in Gambia by Harvard researchers shows that interest rates and even the base perception of the 'time value of money' are significantly affected by the cultural patterns of the economic actors" (Laura Bailey, personal communication, July 1993).

10. "I see an open foreign exchange regime as probably the one key policy for growth" (Roemer et al. 1991).

BIBLIOGRAPHY

Andriamananjara, R., and E. M. Pernia. 1992. “Expansion of Human Amenities, Aptitudes and Skills.” Presented at U.N. interregional symposium, “Promoting Accelerated Development in Africa: Perspectives from the Asian Experience,” Abidjan, Côte d'Ivoire, June 15–19.

Anheier, Helmut K. 1992. “Economic Environments and Differentiation: A Comparative Study of Informal Sector Economies in Nigeria.” *World Development* 20, no. 11: pp. 1,573–85.

Asian Development Bank. 1991. *Asian Development Outlook 1991.* Manila: Asian Development Bank.

Baldwin, Robert. 1992. “Development Experience in Africa and Asia: an Overview.” Presented at U.N. interregional symposium, “Promoting Accelerated Development in Africa: Perspectives from the Asian Experience,” Abidjan, Côte d'Ivoire, June 15–19.

Berger, Peter L., and Hsin-huang Hsiao, ed. 1988. *In Search of an East Asian Development Model.* New Brunswick, N.J.: Transaction Books.

Bruton, Henry. 1992. “Barriers and Opportunities in African Development.” Mimeo, Harvard Institute for International Development.

Cole, David, and James S. Duesenberry. 1992. “Asian Lessons in Finance for Africa.” Mimeo, Harvard Institute for International Development.

Diallo, A., and C. H. Lee. 1992. “Government and Promoting Harmonious Development.” Presented at U.N. interregional symposium, “Promoting Accelerated Development in Africa: Perspectives from the Asian Experience,” Abidjan, Côte d'Ivoire, June 15–19.

Dollar, David. 1992. ''Outward-oriented Developing Economies Really Do Grow More Rapidly: Evidence from 95 LDCs, 1976–1985.'' *Economic Development and Cultural Change* 40, no. 3: pp. 523–44.

Fafchamps, Marcel. 1992. ''The Informal Sector in Africa: Why It Is What It Is.'' Mimeo, Stanford University Food Research Institute.

Fosu, Augustin Kwasi. 1990. ''Exports and Economic Growth: The African Case.'' *World Development* 18, no. 6: pp. 831–35.

Glewwe, Paul. 1991. *Schooling, Skills, and the Returns to Government Investment in Education: An Exploration Using Data for Ghana.* Washington, D.C.: The World Bank.

Global Coalition for Africa. 1992. *African Social and Economic Trends.* 1992 Annual Report. Washington, D.C.: Global Coalition for Africa.

Goldman, Richard H. 1994. ''Patterns and Sources of Food Systems Development.'' In *Asia and Africa: Legacies and Opportunities in Development,* ed. by David L. Lindauer and Michael Roemer. San Francisco: ICS Press.

Grabowski, Richard. 1991. ''Economic Development and the Traditional Sector: A Comparison of Japanese and African Experience.'' *The Developing Economies* XXIX, no. 1: pp. 3–18.

Grey-Johnson, Crispin. 1992. ''The African Informal Sector at the Crossroads: Emerging Policy Options.'' *Africa Development* XVII, no. 1: pp. 65–91.

Hill, Hal. 1993. ''Southeast Asian Economic Development: An Analytical Survey.'' Economics Division Working Papers, Research School of Pacific Studies, Australian National University, Canberra, Australia.

Ikhide, Sylvanus I. 1992. ''Financial Deepening, Credit Availability and the Efficiency of Investment: Evidence from Selected African Countries.'' Research Paper no. 2, Development Research Papers Series, Socio-Economic Research and Planning Division, United Nations Economic Commission for Africa, Addis Ababa, Ethiopia.

International Montary Fund. 1992. *International Financial Statistics Yearbook.* Volume XLV. Washington, D.C.: International Montary Fund.

James, William E. 1990. ''The Transformation of Rural Asia and Economic Development Theory and Policy.'' In *Economic Development in East and Southeast Asia: Essays in Honor of Professor Shinichi Ichimura,* ed. by Seiji Naya and Akira Takayama. Honolulu: East-West Center; Singapore: Institute of Southeast Asian Studies.

James, William E., Seiji Naya, and Gerald M. Meier. 1989. *Asian Development: Economic Success and Policy Lessons.* Madison: University of Wisconsin Press.

Jaycox, Edward V. K. 1992. *The Challenges of African Development.* Washington, D.C.: The World Bank.

Johnson, D. Gale. 1990. *The People's Republic of China: 1978–1990.* San Francisco: ICS Press.

Johnson, D. Gale, Ronald D. Lee, et al. 1986. *Population Growth and Economic Development: Policy Questions.* Washington, D.C.: National Academy Press.

Naya, Seiji, and Pearl Imada. 1992. ''Economic Success of the NIEs and ASEAN: Some Lessons for Latin America?'' In *Southeast Asian Affairs 1992,* pp. 44–57. Singapore: Institute of Southeast Asian Studies.

Nowak, Maria. 1989. ''Financing the Traditional Economy in Africa.'' *The Courier* no. 117: pp. 68–71.

Nzemen, Moise. 1989. ''Tontines and Banking.'' *The Courier* no. 117: pp. 72–73.

Olowu, Dele. 1993. ''The African Economic Crisis and the Governance Question.'' Presented at the International Center for Economic Growth ''Seminar on Effective Implementation of Policies for Growth and Development in Africa,'' Abidjan, Côte D'Ivoire, April 20–24.

Oyowe, Augustine. 1993. ''The Informal Sector: Development at the Grassroots.'' *The Courier* no. 137: pp. 79–80.

Pagni, Lucien. 1992. ''Senegal: The Economy, Heavily Dependent on the Outside World.'' *The Courier* no. 136: pp. 30–32.

Paisley, Ed. 1993. ''Don't Bank on It: Seoul's Reforms Could Give Government Upper Hand.'' *Far Eastern Economic Review,* June 10: p. 67.

Ranis, Gustav. 1991. ''Taiwan as a Classic Model of Asian Development Success.'' In Winrock International 1991, pp. 23–48.

Relecom, Michel. 1993. "Give Priority to Free Enterprise." Interview, *The Courier* no. 137: pp. 81–84.

Richburg, Keith B. 1992. "Why Is Black Africa Overwhelmed While East Asia Overcomes?" *International Herald Tribune,* July 14: p. 6.

Robinson, Peter B., and Somsak Tambunlertchai. 1992. "Stimulation of Production for Domestic Use and Export." Presented at U.N. interregional symposium, "Promoting Accelerated Development in Africa: Perspectives from the Asian Experience," Abidjan, Côte d'Ivoire, June 15–19.

Roemer, Michael. 1993. "What Is Asia's Legacy for African Development?" Presented at the International Center for Economic Growth "Seminar on Effective Implementation of Policies for Growth and Development in Africa," Abidjan, Côte d'Ivoire, April 20–24.

Roemer, Michael, Peter Timmer, Vernon Ruttan, and Linda Lim. 1991. "What Are the Key Lessons from Asian Development Success Stories?" In Winrock International 1991, pp. 49–103.

Roemer, Michael, Thomas Tomich, and Jeffrey Vincent. 1993. "Primary Exports and Industrialization: Development from a Traditional Resource Base." Mimeo, Harvard Institute for International Development.

Salami, Z. K., and A. Tan. 1992. "Augmentation of Capital Formation and Development Finance." Presented at U.N. interregional symposium, "Promoting Accelerated Development in Africa: Perspectives from the Asian Experience," Abidjan, Côte d'Ivoire, June 15–19.

Society for International Development. 1991. "The Challenge of Africa in the 1990s." North South Roundtable Session summary, Ottawa, Canada, June 18–19.

Stoneman, Colin, and Carol B. Thompson. 1991. "Southern Africa after Apartheid: Economic Repercussions of a Free South Africa." *African Recovery* Briefing Paper, December.

Streeten, Paul. 1991. "Social Development in Africa: A Focus on People." *Development,* December: pp. 33–39.

Summers, Robert, and Alan Heston. 1991. "The Penn World Tables

(Mark 5): An Expanded Set of International Comparisons, 1950–1988.'' *Quarterly Journal of Economics* 106, no. 2: pp. 327–68.

Sweden Ministry of Foreign Affairs. 1992. *In Support of Asian Development.* A study commissioned by the Department for International Development Cooperation, Ministry of Foreign Affairs, Stockholm, Sweden.

United Nations. 1992. *World Economic Survey, 1992: Current Trends and Policies in the World Economy.* New York: United Nations Department of Economic and Social Development.

United Nations Development Program. 1992. *Human Development Report 1992.* New York: Oxford University Press.

United Nations, Economic Commission for Africa. 1991. *African Alternative Framework.* Addis Ababa: UNECA.

Winrock International. 1991. *African Development: Lessons from Asia.* Proceedings from a seminar on ''Strategies for the Future of Africa,'' sponsored by the Africa Bureau, U.S. Agency for International Development, and Winrock International at the Radisson Plaza Lord Baltimore Hotel, Baltimore, Maryland, June 5–7.

World Bank. 1985. *China: Agriculture to the Year 2000.* Annex to *China: Long-Term Development Issues and Options.* Washington, D.C.: World Bank.

———. 1992. *World Development Report 1992.* New York: Oxford University Press.

Yaker, Layashi. 1992. ''Preliminary Assessment of the Performance of the African Economy in 1992 and Prospects for 1993.'' End-of-year statement, United Nations Undersecretary General, Executive Secretary of the Economic Commission for Africa, Addis Ababa, December 18.

Young, Robert C. 1992. ''Enterprise Scale, Economic Policy and Development: Evidence on Policy Biases, Firm Size, Efficiency and Growth.'' Presented at U.N. interregional symposium, ''Promoting Accelerated Development in Africa: Perspectives from the Asian Experience,'' Abidjan, Côte d'Ivoire, June 15–19.

Younger, Stephen D. 1992. ''Aid and the Dutch Disease: Macroeconomic Management When Everybody Loves You.'' *World Development* 20, no. 11: pp. 1,587–97.